CORNISH WALKS

TOP WALKS IN MID CORNWALL

CW00552087

LIZ HURLEY

MUDLARK'S PRESS

First Edition, 2019

ISBN: 978-0-9932180-6-4

All maps in this publication are reproduced from Ordnance Survey 1:25,000 maps, with the permission of The Controller of Her Majesty's Stationery Office, Crown copyright.

Map Locations by Google

Coloured Illustrations by Aza Adlam

Bolster illustration by George Cruikshank

Photography by Liz Hurley

A CIP catalogue record for this book is available from the British Library.

Mudlark's Press

www.lizhurleywrites.com

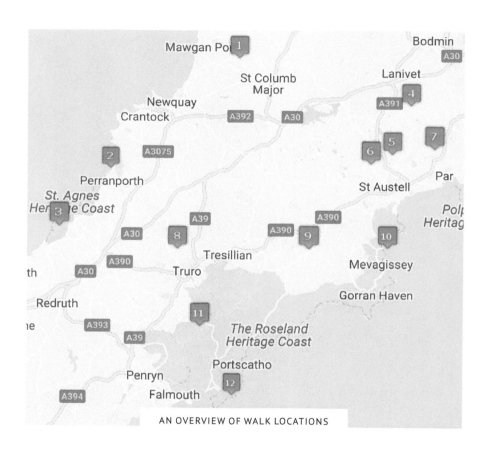

AN OVERVIEW OF WALK LOCATIONS

CONTENTS

INTRODUCTION

Welcome to Top Walks in Cornwall. This series is designed to show you the very best parts of Cornwall and features a wide range of walks.

These walks have been extensively tested and are widely praised for their ease of use and accuracy. Nearly all the walks are circular so you can walk in either direction, although the guide only explains the route one way. If you want a longer walk, just turnaround and retrace your footsteps for a change of scenery. Some of the shorter walks have a neighbouring walk that they can be linked to.

If you do all the walks and their extensions in this book, you will have walked over 60 miles. You will have travelled past Roman forts and Tudor castles, walked the paths of ancient saints, followed streams and rivers down to the sea and beyond. You will have stood in the place of lost estates and hidden wonders and hopefully also spotted some Cornish wildlife as well.

As these are largely countryside / coastal walks, the majority will not be suitable for wheelchairs or buggies.

Each walk is accompanied by notes about various attractions along the route. These interesting snippets help bring the walk to life. The guide also recommends other nearby attractions as well as great places to eat and drink locally.

At the back of the book, there are some bonus features, to enhance your walks. Ranging from recipes, recommended reads and local histories.

Added Extras

In this day and age, a book can only be enhanced by adding in hyperlinks. Each walk features links to further information, as well as a photo gallery of sights from the walk. In the print book, I have shortened long hyperlinks for ease of typing but have left easily typed hyperlinks as they are. In the e-book all links are active.

TIPS AND ADVICE

COUNTRYSIDE CODE

- Respect the people who live and work in the countryside. Respect private property, farmland and all rural environments.

- Do not interfere with livestock, machinery and crops.

- Respect and, where possible, protect all wildlife, plants and trees.

- When walking, use the approved routes and keep as closely as possible to them.

- Take special care when walking on country roads.

- Leave all gates as you find them and do not interfere with or damage any gates, fences, walls or hedges.

- Guard against all risks of fire, especially near forests.

- Always keep children closely supervised while on a walk.

- Do not walk the Ways in large groups and always maintain a low profile.

- Take all litter home - leaving only footprints behind.

- Keep the number of cars used to the minimum and park carefully to avoid blocking farm gateways or narrow roads.

- Minimise impact on fragile vegetation and soft ground.

- Take heed of warning signs - they are there for your protection.

Cattle

- If you find yourself in a field of suddenly wary cattle, move away as carefully and quietly as possible, and if you feel threatened by cattle then let go of your dog's lead and let it run free rather than try to protect it and endanger yourself. The dog will outrun the cows, and it will also outrun you.

- Those without canine companions should follow similar advice: move away calmly, do not panic and make no sudden noises. Chances are the cows will leave you alone once they establish that you pose no threat.

- If you walk through a field of cows and there happen to be calves, be vigilant, as mothers can be more protective. If crossing a field with cattle in, you don't need to stick to the footpath if you wish to avoid them. By all means, skirt around the edge of the field.

- Remain quiet. Cows are curious, if they hear a lot of noise they will come over and investigate.

GUIDE TO THE LEGEND

Before heading off for a walk read the description first. You may discover issues with it. Cows, tides, number of stiles, mud etc. Then have a look at a map, not just the little one provided with the walk, to get a proper feel for the direction of the walk.

LENGTH: This has been calculated using a range of GPS tracking devices but ultimately we have used the Ordnance Survey route tracker. This will generally differ from a pedometer.

EFFORT: Easy to Challenging. These descriptions are only in relation to each other in this book. Every walk has at least one hill in it; not everyone finds hills easy. Challenging, this is for the hardest walks in the book, it will be based on effort and duration. However, nothing in here is particularly tortuous.

TERRAIN: If it's been raining a lot, please assume that footpaths will be muddy. Coast paths tend to be a bit better, near villages they tend to be a bit worse. During the end of summer, vegetation may obscure the path.

FOOTWEAR: I usually walk in walking boots, trainers or ridge sole welling-tons. Except for village walks, smart shoes, sandals, heels or flip flops are unsuitable. Crocs are always unsuitable.*

LIVESTOCK: It is possible that you won't encounter any livestock on a walk that mentions them. Please read the Countryside Code section, on how to avoid them if you do.

PARKING: Postcode for sat nav given. Be aware Cornwall is not always kind to sat navs, have a road map to hand and check you know where you are heading before you set off.

WCs: Due to council cuts, lots of loos are now closed or run by local parishes with seasonal opening hours. If they are an essential part of your walk, check online first. Lots are now coin operated.

CAFÉ / PUB: Local recommendations. Always check ahead, some will have seasonal opening hours.

OS MAP: This will be the largest scale available for the area.

NEARBY ATTRACTIONS: These are sites worth visiting within a short drive of the walk's location. Some will be seasonal and may have an admission charge.

BRIEF DESCRIPTION: Just a quick outline of the walk.

DIRECTIONS: If I say, "going up the road" up or down means there is a slope. If I refer to North or SW, you will need a compass. Most smartphones have built-in compasses. It won't be essential as other directions will be given, but it will be an aide. Especially in woodland where there are few other clues.

OPTIONS: Several of the walks have options or alternate routes to avoid mud, cattle, seasonal access etc. You only need to choose one option, but please read the whole section first. It will help to rule out any confusion.

TIDES: Occasionally I refer to the fact that a high spring tide might block the path, this tends to only last for about an hour, every few months, in the early morning or evening. You are unlikely to be hindered but it is worth pointing out.

FINALLY

Things change: Trees fall down, posts get broken, signs become obscured, footpaths can be closed for repair. Do not be alarmed if you can't see a marker.

*JOKE**

**NOT REALLY :D

1

ST MAWGAN AND THE VALE OF LANHERNE

BRIEF DESCRIPTION: A beautiful and easy figure eight walk, looping through the village of St Mawgan, up and down the *Vale of Lanherne*.

LENGTH: 4.5 miles
EFFORT: Easy
TERRAIN: Mostly very quiet lanes and footpaths
FOOTWEAR: Trainers will be fine
LIVESTOCK: Potential for cattle, sheep, horses, pheasants. Dogs need to be on a lead for nearly the entire walk.
PARKING: Village car park
WCs: St Mawgan
CAFÉ / PUB: Falcon Inn, St Mawgan. St Mawgan Tearooms
OS MAP: 106

NEARBY ATTRACTIONS: Kernow Chocolate Factory. The Japanese Garden. Bedruthan Steps

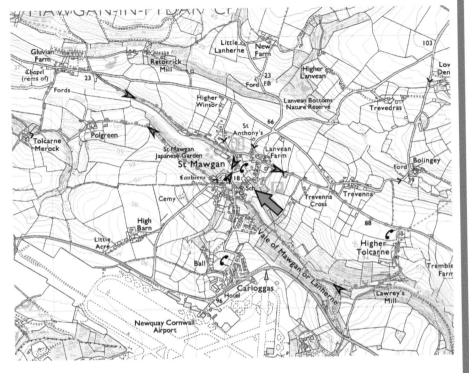

Elevation Profile

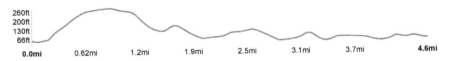

260ft							
200ft							
130ft							
66ft							
0.0mi	0.62mi	1.2mi	1.9mi	2.5mi	3.1mi	3.7mi	**4.6mi**

VALE OF LANHERNE

DIRECTIONS:

1. From the village car park walk out the way you drove in, and out towards the church. At the main road turn right and cross over the bridge. To your right is the village green and to your left, behind the phone box are the public loos. Walk through the village and then turn sharp right at the first junction. Continue uphill until you reach a 30-mph sign and the road bends to the left. Now take the right-hand junction.

2. Continue along this road heading

Vale of Lanherne: Also known as Vale of Mawgan. Lanherne was first mentioned in the Domesday Book and has been the ancestral home for a branch of the powerful Arundell family for many centuries. Originally there was a monastery founded by St Mawgan but this was later converted into a home and the Saxon church beside it was rebuilt in the 1300s.

uphill. It's about three-quarters of a mile and very quiet. Halfway along turn right at a T-junction. The views up here are beautiful.

3.   Turn right at the sign for Higher Tolcarne and walk down through the hamlet. At the end of the lane, follow the public footpath sign leading to Lawrey Mill, this path runs along the side of a few homes and then turns sharply downhill. Follow the footpath towards the valley floor. This section is steep and can be slippery.

4.   When you reach the river, take the left-hand footbridge, and cross over, then turn right. If you wish to explore Lawrey's Mill, turn left and walk along to the

i **Carmelite Convent:** When the French invaded Belgium in 1794 a group of Carmelite nuns fled to England and Henry, the eighth Lord of Arundell offered them Lanherne Manor as their new home. The nuns remained there until 2001 when it was passed over to a Franciscan body of nuns and was recently taken on by the Roman Catholic diocese of Plymouth.

Whilst the Convent is obviously not open to visitors, you may visit the chapel of St Joseph and St Anne on most days. This is

CARMELITE CONVENT

abandoned mill and then return to this point. The path is clear and easy to follow, shortly after the bridge turn right where the paths cross. After a few hundred yards the path opens into a small clearing with a choice of four paths. You need to take attached to the convent on the Church side of the building. Just before the entrance to the chapel is a tenth or eleventh century stone crucifix.

the second on your right. This path heads gently uphill away from the river. Follow the footpath all the way back into the village, head through the kissing gate, and you will find yourself back in the car park.

5.   Again walk out of the car park but this time as you reach the church turn left and walk up towards the *Carmelite convent*. Walk past the Falcon

A COLOURFUL RIVER

Inn and then cross to the other side of the road. Take the footpath up towards the convent, head through the gate and up to the main entrance. There is a public chapel just to the right of the entrance, if you wish to visit, otherwise turn left along the lane keeping the convent walls on your right. Follow the lane as it turns right, on the corner is a small graveyard and further along, on the left-hand wall, you can see the Stations of the Cross and ornate pillars. These are the walls to the convent's private gardens. When the lane reaches the road, turn right and walk downhill. The path continues shortly on your left, through a metal farm gate and along a farmer's track.

6. This track now heads down through three fields and there are often cattle somewhere about.

7. Head through the bottom gate and into a small hamlet. Walk along this lane slowly heading uphill for about half a mile until you see some wooden picket fencing ahead of you. Just past this fencing is an old lane on your right which you need to take.

8. This old lane cuts across the valley floor, at one point you can see all the way down to the sea. Further on are two streams with fords to cross them, after the second ford head back uphill until you reach a road. Turn right and walk for a few hundred metres, passing a holiday complex on your left until you see a footpath sign on your right. This is by a pop-up café.

9. Take the footpath and continue along it until it ends at a private drive, there is one stile along the way. Continue walking along the private drive, passing several residences until it joins the highway. Turn right and walk back into the village of St Mawgan. To return to your car, cross through the village green and on the other side cross the picturesque ford by the village school. The car park is just beyond this to your left.

LINKS:

The Little White Hare of Lanherne
https://www.lizhurleywrites.com/2018/10/09/the-little-white-hare-of-lanherne/

PHOTO ALBUM:

https://flic.kr/s/aHsmrsDZ4v

2

SURFING WITH THE SAINTS

BRIEF DESCRIPTION: A fabulous walk that follows in the footsteps of *St Piran*, one of Cornwall's patron saints, in and around Perranporth and Holywell. Along the way, the trail reveals lots of hidden places that are easily overlooked. Sea caves, geological wonders, hidden lakes, ancient theatres, and churches lost in the dunes. All this and a great choice of pubs.
ADDITIONAL INFORMATION: This walk is best done at low tide and in good weather, the cliff section will be arduous or even dangerous in heavy rain, strong winds or low visibility.
LENGTH: 10 miles
EFFORT: Hard. Most of the walk is easy, but it is a long walk and the section in the dunes and on the coast path can be tiring
TERRAIN: Lanes, fields, sand dunes, beach and coast path
FOOTWEAR: Something sturdy
LIVESTOCK: Highly unlikely
PARKING: Holywell National Trust car park
WCs: Cubert, Holywell
CAFÉ / PUB: Various good options in Cubert & Holywell. The Plume of Feathers at Mitchell is a short drive away and worth it
OS MAP: 104
NEARBY ATTRACTIONS: Trerice House. Lappa Valley Railways. Blue Reef Aquarium, Newquay

Elevation Profile

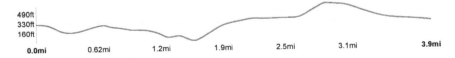

490ft						
330ft						
160ft						
0.0mi	0.62mi	1.2mi	1.9mi	2.5mi	3.1mi	3.9mi

PENHALE SANDS

DIRECTIONS:

1. From the National Trust car park walk along the road back past the loos and up towards the seasonal convenience shop. Take the small road in front of the shop and follow the footpath signs. Turn right and follow the path along the perimeter of the houses. As you walk through the dunes stick to the main path, keeping to the edge of the houses. The path stops at a golf course. Rather than walk onto the course, take the path to the right of the gate. This cuts through scrubland and eventually you will pop out at a small intersection. To your left is a flight of concrete steps, ignore

St Piran: Piran, also known as Perran, was an Irish Saint who was thrown out to sea by the Irish, tied to a millstone. As it hit the water, the waters stilled and so he rode upon the millstone across the Irish seas and landed on the north coast of Cornwall thereby making him the first known Cornish surfer. He is also attributed with rediscovering the smelting of tin and thereby creating the symbol of the Cornish Flag, the white molten

this and walk forward, you will emerge into a small glade with *St Cubert's Holy Well* on your left.

2.   With the holy well behind you, walk past the pond and, with extreme care, out onto the golf course. Walk up the hill sticking closely to the hedge on your right. You will see the flag for the 18th hole ahead and above you. Any ball coming in will be coming from the left, this is only a pitch and put but still, take care. Continue past the green, through the large stone-lined gap in the hedge and walk straight towards the clubhouse. There is no charge to visit the well but there is a charity box in the reception and a small offering may be appropriate. Leave the golf club and head out to the main road. Turn left and walk uphill towards the village of Cubert, there is a pavement the whole way. Walk into the village and into the churchyard.

3.   From Cubert Church tower, head out through the metal kissing gate and take the left-hand footpath. When you reach the road, cross over, turn right, walk a few metres along the road, then walk down the next footpath. At the end of the footpath turn right and at the end of the passage, climb left through the stile into the field.

4.   The view up here is amazing and gives you an idea of the size of Penhale Sands. Walk down the field approximately half way, keeping the hedge on your

tin crossing the black granite smelting block. Whilst St Michael and St Petroc claim to be the official patron saints of Cornwall, St Piran also has this claim, as well as being the patron saint of miners. St Piran's Day is celebrated on March 5th and is generally well celebrated throughout the county.

i **St Cubert's Holy Well:** Tucked in the middle of a golf course is this pretty holy well. Believed to have been built in the fifteenth century it was restored to its former glory in 1936. It is a beautiful spot sitting beside a range of ponds with the natural spring flowing down through the well.

i **Perran Round:** This circular medieval amphitheatre is known as a Plen-an-gwary, a Cornish open-air theatre used for the staging of miracle plays. Perran Round is considered the oldest and best preserved example of its kind. You can still see the Devil's Pan in the centre that would have been used to symbolise the descent into hell. This site was probably an earlier Iron Age enclosure.

immediate right. The path then heads into the undergrowth and continues downhill through trees.

5.   Follow the path until it pops out on a small track. There is a little slip path to the right, down onto the road, take this and once on the road, turn right and walk pass Old Tree Barn on your left. At the end go through the second five-bar gate and turn left, continuing downhill until you reach the valley floor and stream. This whole area is a wetland and is likely to be very boggy in wet weather. Cross the bridge and continue along the path. Go through the kissing gate and head left.

6.   Soon the path comes out onto a large common and continues around its edge.

Sand Dunes: Penhale Sands are the largest complex of sand dunes in Cornwall and are a designated SSSI (Site of Special Scientific Interest). They are stabilised by marram grass, the malevolent spiky grass that stabs away at your legs and the will to live. Once this grass is established, other species begin to take root, further stabilising the sands. Penhale Sands is also the site of the mythical Langarroc, a village that was swallowed by the sands. Legend has it that on windy nights you can still hear the church bells tolling.

PERRAN ROUND

AMONGST THE SAND DUNES

The footpath is initially unclear but stick to the left-hand edge of the common, skirting the scrubland. You are heading towards the electricity pylons on the skyline. After a short while, the path ends at a gate.

7.   Head through the metal gate out onto a lane, turn right and walk uphill. This is a quiet lane and whilst cars do use it, they are slow and there is plenty of room on the verges if you need to step off the road. Walk for about a mile until you reach a white bungalow on your left and the sign for "The Wainhouse" and "Two Hoots Barn" on your right. Walk up the drive towards the bungalow and directly before the white gatepost turn right following the footpath sign.

8.   Follow this footpath into an arable field. Keep the hedge on your immediate right and walk the length of the field heading towards the farm buildings. Just before the buildings, turn right down the track and then take the drive left. This will now bring you to the front of the farm buildings. Now walk downhill, climbing over the stile by the farm gate and continue down the drive.

9.   Follow the drive down to the small road, cross over following the footpath sign and continue on the footpath heading up alongside a cottage called Rose Wollas on the right. The footpath eventually ends at a large track opening into some fields. Turn right and follow the obvious track all

 St Piran's Church, Oratory and Cross: The fact that the cross, St Piran's Church and St Piran's Oratory were all lost to the sands shows how easily the tale of *Langarroc* could be believed. The Oratory is thought to have been built in the sixth or seventh century and was founded by St Piran, this makes it one of the oldest surviving Christian sites in the UK. The encroaching sands meant that the local parishioners decided to build a new church, they abandoned the Oratory and moved the cross to its current site. The Church was then in use up until the nineteenth century

ST PIRAN'S CROSS

when again the battle against the sand was lost. A third church was then built five miles inland. Ironically having been regularly resurrected from the sands during the eighteenth and nineteenth centuries, the council reburied the Oratory in the 1980s to protect it from vandalism. The Oratory was once again resurrected in 2014. Sadly, the little church is now entombed behind iron railings and concrete blocks.

St Piran's Church, possibly dating from the twelfth century is now merely an outline in the ground, but it is at least accessible and beside the site sits an ancient cross, dating from 980 AD. The

PERRANPORTH BEACH

the way until just before the road. There is a wooden fence to your right, climb over the stile and you will find yourself at the mediaeval amphitheatre of *Perran Round*.

10.   Having explored the amphitheatre you now want to exit via the main gate and turn immediately right down an unmade road, through the village of Rose. When the unmade road joins a tarmacked road, turn right and walk out of the village. You are now heading directly towards *St Piran's Oratory*. This road ends at a T-Junction where directly ahead and slightly to the right is a stile in the hedgerow. Head over the stile.

11.   Once over the stile take the right-hand fork and walk into the *sand dune* system. There are many paths that you can take through here, however you need to be moving in a right-hand direction and sticking to the larger paths will achieve this. There are white painted breezeblocks on the floor along the way. Follow these and take the right-hand branch when they split off. As you walk along you will gradually see a large modern cross on the horizon, keep this to your left.

The first feature you will come to is an ancient cross and a sunken church. Standing facing the information plaque, turn immediately left and follow the path downhill. Again, follow the white breeze-blocks and cross over the small wooden bridge, within a minute you will come

church itself was eventually abandoned in the 1800s as the fight against the sands became impossible. Most of the church was torn down and re-used at the site of Lambourne.

Mines: Sometimes it's hard to spot a place in Cornwall that doesn't have a mine. This mine was known as Gravel Hill. It was worked from the seventeenth century until 1882, producing iron and zinc. The shafts, spoil heaps, buildings and trackways associated with this mine are visible on vertical aerial photographs of the area.

Holy Wells - The Sea Cave: As you walk around the headland and first look down on Holywell Bay, there is a sea cave dead ahead of you, on the other side of the beach. It is here that the holy well, from which the Bay gets its name, is located. The cave is easy to reach at low tide but impossible at high tide. There are no lifeguards at that end of the beach so always pay attention to the tide. To find the cave simply walk along the base of the cliff until you get to

SEA VIEWS

across the excavated *Church Oratory*. First impressions are of an abandoned breeze block garage. Up to your left, towering over the landscape is the giant cross.

12.   From either the large cross or the Church Oratory, you need to walk forwards towards the sea. You may come across an MOD fence, do not attempt to cross it, instead head down towards the beach. The descent is sandy and steep but good fun. Once on the beach turn right and walk to the far end. You are now on the coast path. In the far corner of the beach is a sea cave and lake. If you explore the lake area you can see some sealed off shafts into a disused *mine*.

the cave. The well is on the left-hand side, above your head, it is not too far in and easy to see. So long as you are in the right cave. This well appears to have taken advantage of a natural geological formation, fresh water running down through the cliffs have created a natural spring but also left a variety of mineral deposits. These deposits have turned the surrounding rocks into a multicoloured splendour as well as forming shelves of calcium, it is a beautiful sight. Below the well, you can see steps leading up to it,

21

INCREDIBLE NATURAL ROCK FORMATIONS

13.   Leaving the cave behind, return to the coast path and start walking up the dunes. This is steep and tiring but soon you will be at the top with glorious views. Now stick to the coast path with the sea on your left. The next section needs to be walked with care, children and dogs need to be kept under control as you pass fenced off mine shafts, exposed cliff edges and MOD land. This section is about two miles and drops down into Holywell Bay.

14.   Looking across Holywell Bay, there is a sea cave, containing a spectacular holy well. It is at the far side, to the right of an outcrop of rocks. *See notes. Holy*

but these are incredibly slippery, and it is probably best to admire from afar rather than slipping and breaking something. When I visited the well was high above me due to there being little sand in the cave. You may visit when the floor level is much higher. The existence of the well has been mentioned since 1685 when the Cornish historian Hals remarked on its fame and curative properties.

Wells – The Sea Cave. If you would like to go and look at this cave, continue along the coast path and turn left onto the beach just before the St Piran pub. Be aware of the tide.

15. From the beach return to the road and turn right, back towards the car park.

LINKS:

Holy Wells
https://www.nationaltrust.org.uk/holywell/features/hidden-surprises-at-holywell
Lost Land of Langarroc
https://www.lizhurleywrites.com/2019/01/20/lost-lands-warnings-from-the-past/
Penhale Sands
https://en.wikipedia.org/wiki/Penhale_Sands
St Piran - Saint/Oratory/Church/Cross & Round http://stpiran.org
Tide Timetables https://bit.ly/2IOJw9I

PHOTO ALBUM:

https://flic.kr/s/aHskERSRwZ

3

ST AGNES BEACON AND WHEAL COATES

BRIEF DESCRIPTION: An exhilarating and photogenic walk. From the coast path you walk through iconic tin mines, the path then heads up to St Agnes Beacon, with glorious views over the surrounding countryside.

ADDITIONAL INFORMATION: No dogs on the beach between Easter and September. This walk is high up and exposed, it will be no fun in high winds, low clouds or rain.

LENGTH: 3.5 miles

EFFORT: Short but strenuous

TERRAIN: Coast and footpath. One small road

FOOTWEAR: Sturdy. A lot of the footpaths are loose scree and can be slippery

LIVESTOCK: None

PARKING: This is a tricky car park to find and not suitable for tall vehicles, but it is free and large. The postcode TR5 0NU will get you close and then you need to rely on map reading. Head towards the large arrow, marked on the map opposite. It is NOT the nearby NT carpark.

WCs: Chapel Porth Loos (on the route) These are seasonal with limited opening in winter

CAFÉ / PUB: Driftwood Spars, St Agnes. Chapel Porth Café (on the route), this café is seasonal with limited opening in winter

OS MAP: 104

NEARBY ATTRACTIONS: Healey's Cornish Cider Farm

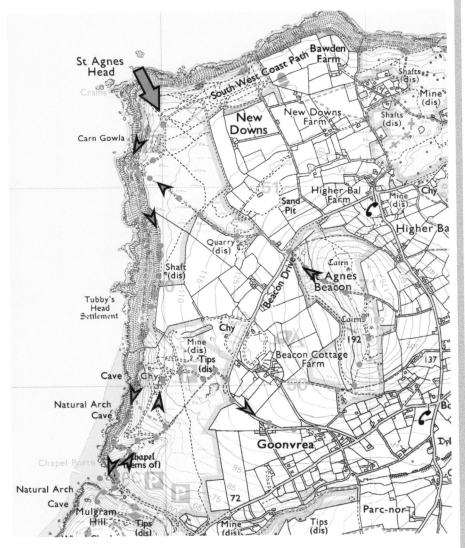

Elevation Profile

490ft						
330ft						
160ft						
0.0mi	0.62mi	1.2mi	1.9mi	2.5mi	3.1mi	3.9mi

TOWANROATH SHAFT ENGINE HOUSE

DIRECTIONS:

1. From the car park walk towards the sea and take any path heading left, they will gradually all lead to the coast path which you should follow until you pass a capped off mine shaft. Shortly after this the path splits, take the lower right-hand fork. This is marked with a small wooden post as the coast path. Walk along until you get to Towanroath Shaft *Engine House*, the lower mine at *Wheal Coates*. Having explored the Engine House, continue along the coast path with the sea on your right.

NOTE: We will come back this way later which will provide the opportunity to

Wheal Coates: In 2006 the Cornish and Devon Mining heritage sites were designated as a UNESCO World Heritage Site. With its dramatic location, Wheal Coates is one of the outstanding jewels in the crown. Tin mining had been performed on this site for many centuries, but it became an industrial endeavour on a global scale in 1802. As mines like this and others around Cornwall closed down, the miners and their families headed out across the seas taking their skills and

explore the other buildings higher up the hill.

2.   When the path reaches a large outcrop of rocks overlooking the beach, you will need to take the footpath down to the beach if you wish to visit the café and loos. You should then return to this coast path when you come back off the beach.

3.   Whilst on the path down to the beach keep an eye out for the ruined St Agnes Chapel and nearby a rock that bears the imprint of one of the giant *Bolster's* fingers. Down on the beach if you see any red stained rocks, know that that is Bolster's blood!

4.   Having explored the beach, you need to retrace your footsteps to the top path. You are now leaving the coast path. There are a few routes up, but whichever you choose, make sure that you are on the left side of the valley with the sea behind you. At one point a small path intersects this path. Turn left up into the heather and gorse. You are now effectively walking back on yourself from the earlier coast path, this time however you are a few hundred metres inland.

5.   The path you are on now leads back along to the higher part of Wheal Coates, a large collection of mining buildings, that are great to explore. Having had a

knowledge with them and were the world's pre-eminent miners. Through Cornish blood, sweat, tears and pasties a global industrial revolution continued to grow.

EV Thompson once joked that it didn't matter where you went in the world, if you came upon a mine shaft there'd be a Cornishman at the bottom. His point was made in a South African gem mine where he bumped into two men from Camborne and Redruth.

Engine Houses: An engine house is a very iconic building. Generally, three or four stories tall it would be attached to an even taller chimney. They were built to house massive steam-driven, pump engines that were responsible for keeping the shafts clear of water so that they could be properly mined. The mine shafts themselves would be very close to the engine house. If you look around, you will start to realise just how many mines there are in this area and what an incredible sight it must have been during the height of the mining industry.

look, take the large path away from the site heading inland towards the large hill (*St Agnes Beacon*) ahead of you. The path leads to a National Trust car park. Walk through this and out onto the road, then turn right.

6. Follow the road for about 600m until you get to Mor Cliff Holiday complex on your right. Walk past Porth Vale house and take the unpaved road opposite their drive, that points directly up to the beacon.

7. Follow this lane up and when it bends to the right, take the footpath on

Bolster - The St Agnes Giant: Enjoy the full story at the back of this book, under Extra Helpings.

St Agnes Beacon and Bolster's Bank: Bolster's Bank is a substantial linear earthwork. There are some suggestions that it may once have been much longer, totally enclosing the Beacon and St Agnes Head. In much the same way as Dodman Point on the south coast, this is another small

VIEW FROM ST AGNES BEACON

the left that heads directly up towards the electricity pylons. This section is steep but the view from the top is sudden and magnificent. You are now 192 metres above sea level and it's all downhill from here. The top of the beacon is marked by a trig point and a toposcope. From here you can also spot *Bolster's Bank*, it's nearby but hard to make out. The many tin mines are far easier to spot.

8.   From the trig point walk straight down on the obvious path, and where the path forks, take the left-hand path.

9.   Follow this path all the way down off the hill. When you reach the road, cross over and walk down the lane opposite. You are now heading back towards your car. When you get to the army sentry box on your right, head left through a small lay-by area and follow the footpath sign heading along an abandoned road. There are ruined structures to either side of you and the footpath leads on over a set of stone steps. Follow this path through the gorse and heather back to the car park.

headland protected from the sea by tall cliffs. The Beacon itself was the site of an Iron Age hillfort and various cairns, although these are now hard to make out on the ground.

BOLSTER'S BLOOD

LINKS:

Cornish Tin Mining https://bit.ly/2UPv1Z2
Wheal Coates https://bit.ly/2LiKw7H

PHOTO ALBUM:

https://flic.kr/s/aHsmjUN7sw

4

HELMAN TOR

BRIEF DESCRIPTION: A peaceful walk along tiny country lanes then leading into a nature reserve and up onto a tor with magnificent views before heading down to one of the area's finest pubs.

LENGTH: 6 miles
EFFORT: Easy. Only the climb up to the Tor is in any way challenging
TERRAIN: Mostly very quiet lanes and footpaths
FOOTWEAR: Sections of this walk can be extremely wet. Climbing about on the Tor requires good soles, trainers minimum, walking boots better. If the weather has been wet I would recommend wellies.
LIVESTOCK: Potential for cattle, sheep, horses, wildfowl. Dogs need to be on a lead for most sections.
PARKING: The Crown Inn, Lanlivery
WCs: The Crown Inn, Lanlivery
CAFÉ / PUB: The Crown Inn, Lanlivery
OS MAP: 107

NEARBY ATTRACTIONS: Lostwithiel. Lanhydrock House. Roche Rock (dramatic hermitage). Castel an Dinas (impressive iron age hillfort)

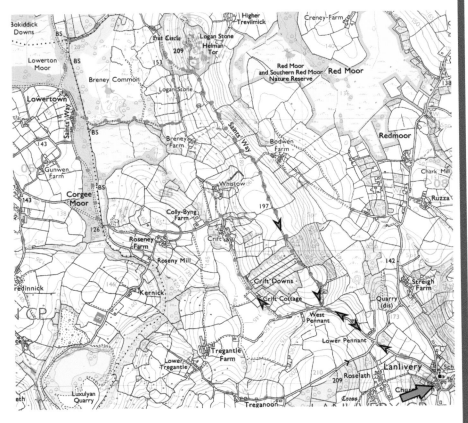

Elevation Profile

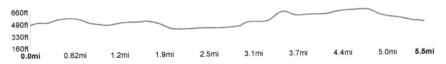

660ft									
490ft									
330ft									
160ft									
0.0mi	0.62mi	1.2mi	1.9mi	2.5mi	3.1mi	3.7mi	4.4mi	5.0mi	5.5mi

HELMAN TOR

DIRECTIONS:

1. From the car park turn immediately left following the sign Luxulyan, when you get to a staggered crossroad, continue straight on. Stay on this road for about 2 miles by which time it will have become a very quiet lane.

2. As you walk along the lane look into the fields on either side and you will spot many giant boulders of granite for which this area is well known. When you reach Whistow Farm, after about a mile, the lane heads left, gradually heading downhill. After about a half mile the landscape changes to bog land and can be very

Cornish Wildlife: Helman Tor, Brenney Common and other neighbouring Commons are all nature reserves and sit in the centre of several sites of scientific interest. That means there are lots of rare and unusual flora and fauna to keep an eye out for, including marsh fritillary butterflies and sundew carnivorous plants.

atmospheric, with mossy trees, streams and pools. Continue along the lane until it enters a small hamlet with a few homes on the left.

3.   After the second property, take the footpath on the right of the lane. There is a signpost pointing to the Wilderness Trail, cross over the stream, through the gate and onto Brenney Common. I often come across cattle here, but they are lovely and will always go out of their way to avoid you.

4.   Having entered the nature reserve, you need to stick to the path you are on, continuing straight and ignore any branches off to the sides. At the granite sign-stone make sure you stick to the right-hand major fork. Proceed through two more metal gates until you start to climb out of the nature reserve.

5.   The path ends at a T-junction at which point, turn left and walk along the track until it joins a small tarmacked road. Helman Tor is right ahead of you. Turn right onto the road and walk uphill until you get to the car park on your left.

6.   From the car park walk up onto the Tor and enjoy the views. When rested, head back down to the car park and now turn left along the road. The tarmac peters out almost straight away and you are now on a track which you should continue along for just over a mile. This track is

i **Cornish Tors:** A tor is a large, free-standing rock outcrop that rises abruptly from the surrounding smooth and gentle slopes of a rounded hill summit or ridge crest. Tors are landforms created by the erosion and weathering of rock; most commonly granites, but also schists, dacites, dolerites, coarse sandstones and others. Tors are mostly less than 5 metres (16 ft) high. Each outcrop can comprise several tiers or pillows, which may become separated stacks: rocking pillows are called logan stones. These stacks are vulnerable to frost action and often collapse leaving trails of blocks down the slopes called *clitter* or *clatter*. Weathering has also given rise to circular "rock basins" formed by the accumulation of water and repeated freezing and thawing. (Source: Wiki).

i **The Saints' Way:** During the early spread of Christianity from Ireland and the Scottish communities, there was a lot of traffic along the western edge of the British Isles. Saints travelled between Scotland, Ireland, Wales, Cornwall and Brittany. There is evidence all

part of the *Saints' Way*. It is prone to mud and at times can become seriously waterlogged in places. At the worst point, the water can be deeper than walking boots or little wellies. Happily, there is a diversion.

7.   When you pass two metal five bar gates, one on each side of the track, you are about to meet the "pond". In dry weather, this isn't an issue. But this is Cornwall. If you can walk on without impediment, do so. If you are facing a lake, take the wooden kissing gate on your right, into the field. Turn left and walk along the hedge, passing into the second field and then exiting at the top left-hand corner and re-joining the track. There are often moorland ponies in these two fields.

over Cornwall of the impact that the saints had on the land; there are more saint place names in Cornwall than anywhere else in Britain. These holy men and women were clearly passing through Cornwall and whilst an actual path was never known, one could be guessed at. In the late 1990s, a Saints Way across Cornwall, connecting important religious sites from the fifth century, was established. Of course, it wouldn't just have been Saints using these paths. Cornwall was rich in tin, which had fuelled the Bronze Age and there is evidence of the tin trade stretching as far as the Phoenician

FRIENDLY NEIGHBOURS

NATURE RESERVE

trading routes. Ireland and Wales were also rich in gold so there would have been many merchants. One story claims that Joseph of Arimathea came to Cornwall to trade in tin and that one of his companions was Jesus himself. Whilst the legitimacy of this claim is weak, the fact that the story exists, lends evidence to the importance of Cornwall, as a place of great resources and international trading, for the past two thousand years.

8.   Now continue along the track. Looking forward, you should be able to see the distinctive tower of Lanlivery Church. Gradually the path starts to head downhill until it joins a road. This was the road you started out on. Turn left and head back to the pub for a glass of something cold and a bowl of something warm.

LINKS:

The Cornwall Wildlife Trust http://www.cornwallwildlifetrust.org.uk/

PHOTO ALBUM:

https://flic.kr/s/aHsmxtVBFt

5

EDEN TRAILS 1

BRIEF DESCRIPTION: An easy walk through a modern industrial landscape, there are lots of opportunities for dogs to wander free and explore. Walk through the remnants of a *china clay mining industry* whose alien landscape has been used as a location for Doctor Who. This walk can be combined with the Sky Trail walk.

LENGTH: 6 miles
EFFORT: Easy
TERRAIN: Cycle and footpath
FOOTWEAR: Trainers. Some wet sections after heavy rain
LIVESTOCK: None
PARKING: PL26 8TX. This car park has been created by the closure of a road so old sat navs may get fooled trying to find it. You need to head to Carluddon and from the mini roundabout head down the No Through Road
WCs: None
CAFÉ / PUB: Closest pub The Carclaze
OS MAP: 107

NEARBY ATTRACTIONS: Eden Project. Charlestown Shipwreck Centre. Pinetum Gardens. China Clay Museum

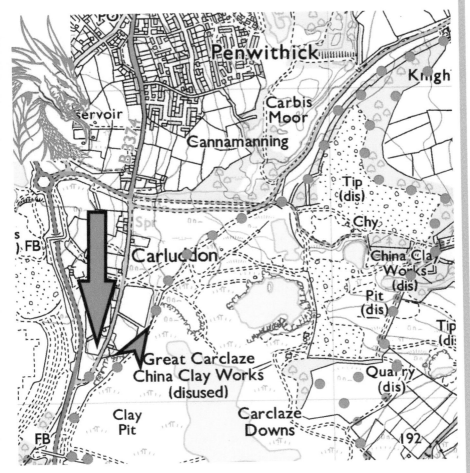

Elevation Profile

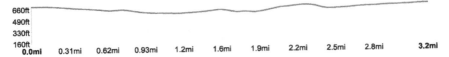

660ft										
490ft										
330ft										
160ft										

0.0mi 0.31mi 0.62mi 0.93mi 1.2mi 1.6mi 1.9mi 2.2mi 2.5mi 2.8mi 3.2mi

LOOKING TOWARD THE PYRAMIDS

DIRECTIONS:

1. From the car park, with the pyramid behind you turn right and walk towards the road bridge, then turn left onto a lower unmade footpath and start walking left down the loose surface. Walk along the path with a large open-cast mining pit to your right. Dogs are fine off the lead. The path beneath your feet is mostly made of mica, a by-product of the mining industry as the majority of this walk is on reclaimed land. Go through the small wooden gate and continue forwards. Here the path comes to an obvious T-junction, turn left towards a waist-high wooden

Modern China Clay Industry: Cornwall is the third largest exporter of Kaolin (china clay) in the world and was once the leading exporter after China, before other global deposits were found. It is hydrologically mined, this means that high-pressure water cannons are shot at the rock face to extract the kaolin as a water-based slurry. The slurry is then taken off to the dries. China clay is a global industry and is used in a vast range of products, from medicine

post and then turn right, and with the pyramid behind you, start walking down the path.

2.   As you walk along this path keep an eye out for fence posts ahead. If you have an exuberant or "deaf" dog that doesn't like to walk to heal, then this would be a good moment to put them on their lead as the path moves towards the road and car park.

3.   Head through the kissing gate at the fence posts and go straight across the wide path and onto a small footpath heading into the trees. This footpath runs alongside a road for this section. There is plenty of room to the right for your dog to explore but if you are not confident, keep them on a lead. Continue along this footpath for another half a mile, this section can be muddy after heavy rain but it's also a great spot for blackberries. As the path starts to rise put your dog on the lead as the path ends at another kissing gate by a car park and road.

4.   Go through this kissing gate and turn right, then walk through two large metal gates. Dogs are now fine off the lead for the rest of the walk. Follow the path through scrubland, ahead of you, you can see a ridge which you will soon be walking along.

5.   When you get to the next set of gates, head through the far-left set and

FIELDS OF FOXGLOVES

ENJOYING THE VIEW

39

walk towards the fence on your right. Start walking up the ridge alongside the fence, you are now walking on a massive spoil heap. The views up here are spectacular, behind you, in clear weather, you can see onto Bodmin Moor. Follow the fence on your right, all the way along until you come back off the heap. Ahead of you, you can see a wide white path, which is your next route.

6.   Continue down on the current path. As you leave the fence you now join National Cycle Trail, Route 2. Walk forwards and go through a metal gate, there is now a long hill in front of you, walk to the top. Turn left at the T-junction at the top, following the cycle trail and then just where the bushes end, turn right, leaving the cycle trail and take the steep grassy path up the hill. As you get to the spine of the hill turn right and carry on up until you reach the *stone circle* at the top. Walk through the stones towards the fence and have a look down at some of the pits.

7.   Now return through the stones, and as you pass the king stone, a large boulder on its own, turn right and take the grass path back down the hill overlooking St Austell Bay. At the bottom rejoin the cycle path and turn right. From here you will circumnavigate Baal Pit, ignore any left-hand turns. You can see why this location was used for a Doctor Who episode,

to coating paper. It is an industry that has literally changed the face of Cornwall bringing wealth and opportunities to an otherwise impoverished area.

i   Stone Circle: This is a modern stone circle that was built by English China Clay when they landscaped this hill. It's a nice thought that for whatever reason the Cornish are still building stone circles.

THE CLAY FIELDS

SUNSET AT THE STONE CIRCLE

Colony in Space. It's also worth considering that whilst it looks barren and alien, this is exactly what the *Eden Project* looked like before it was transformed. Walk past a shelter with some benches and continue along the path.

8.   As you approach a road bridge put your dog back on the lead.

If you want to extend this walk climb the steps, cross the road via the bridge and follow the instructions for the Sky Trail walk. Otherwise, turn right and walk back to your car.

LINKS:

A Brief History of China Clay
https://www.cornwalls.co.uk/history/industrial/china_clay.htm
The Clay Trails http://www.claytrails.co.uk/
The Eden Project https://www.edenproject.com

PHOTO ALBUM:

https://flic.kr/s/aHsmaY1DEm

41

6

EDEN TRAILS 2 - SKY TRAIL

BRIEF DESCRIPTION: A short walk with excellent views over the china clay mines. Great for dogs, although pay attention to cyclists. This walk can be combined with the Eden Trails 1 walk.

LENGTH: 2.5 miles
EFFORT: Easy
TERRAIN: Well-drained footpath and cycle path
FOOTWEAR: Any
LIVESTOCK: None
PARKING: There is a small car park just beyond a new housing estate. PL25 5RY. A larger car park is available across the main A road and accessed via a footbridge (PL26 8TX)
WCs: None
CAFÉ / PUB: On the other side of the large roundabout is the pub, The Carclaze Arms
OS MAP: 107

NEARBY ATTRACTIONS: Eden Project. Charlestown Shipwreck Centre. Pinetum Gardens. China Clay Museum

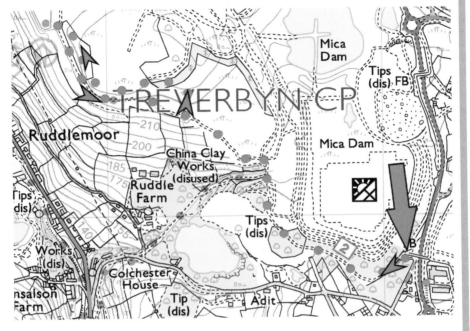

Elevation Profile

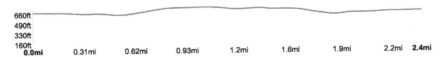

660ft								
490ft								
330ft								
160ft								
0.0mi	0.31mi	0.62mi	0.93mi	1.2mi	1.6mi	1.9mi	2.2mi	2.4mi

LOOKING OVER ST AUSTELL BAY

DIRECTIONS:

Due to the close proximity of the A391 make sure your dog is on a lead when you get out of the car.

1. From the car park walk towards the footbridge and then turn left. You are now on National Cycle Trail, Route 2. It isn't a busy route but there will be cyclists especially in summer. Follow the path to the left and keep on it for about half a mile, at which point it has two left-hand turnings close to each other.

2. For a small diversion turn left at the second turning and head downhill. As the path turns left again, walk forward past two large granite boulders into the

China Clay Industry: For centuries China dominated the porcelain industry, exporting it to Europe where it was in high demand as the local product, fine stoneware was an inferior product. In 1745 William Cookworthy was determined to locate a source of kaolin outside of China and found a deposit in Cornwall. He began to refine it and triggered an industry in Cornwall, and the St Austell area in particular that became a global market which has continued for the next two

undergrowth. The slope now leads down to a small stream. This is a nice source of fresh water for dogs but it is also a nice example of two streams of two different colours converging, one is red from tin or iron, one is white from china clay. After heavy rain, the difference is quite noticeable.

3.   Return up to the main path and continue to walk forwards. The path, which begins to rise gently, is now part of the Sky Trail Spur and not part of Cycle Route 2. After a while, you will see on your right a hut with a footpath leading off behind it.

This following section is short and steep but gives amazing views over the surrounding countryside. Alternatively,

hundred and fifty years. It has shaped almost everything that you can see in this area of Cornwall.

i **White Pyramids:** One of the most dramatic impacts the china clay industry has had has been on the skyline around St Austell. Looking around you can see lots of large pyramid structures, the largest of which is just above Carluddon. These are tips or slag heaps from the refining process. Once they were all white, earning them the nickname of the Cornish Alps now only the largest remains a whiteish grey, as the others have been terraformed and re-seeded.

AN INDUSTRIAL SKYLINE

you can continue along the main path as this smaller path will rejoin it later on.

4.   As the small path climbs it will turn to the left along a wire fence then open onto a plateau. From the summit, you can now walk along the spine of this clay tip. Looking down to your left you can see the sky trail spur. The landscape up here is littered with the remains of centuries of the *china clay industry*. Behind you is a giant grey triangular tip, to your left are small green pyramids. Collectively these were known as the *White Pyramids*. As you look down you can see incredible *turquoise coloured lakes* and as you

Turquoise Lakes: Until you see these strange green lakes it's hard to appreciate how unusual they are. Ranging from milky blues to glowing emerald these lakes contain water rich in mica and copper mineral deposits, a residue from the washing of the clay. The water is perfectly safe, but swimming is forbidden. These are not naturally formed lakes; they are hollowed out pits meaning the sides are sheer, they are extremely deep and very cold.

TURQUOISE COLOURED LAKES

walk along the spine, you can see the open-cast mining in the hillside ahead of you, across the valley. Carry along the spine, taking care as the path can be uneven and very windy, until the path gradually heads back down and rejoins the cycle path. As you come off the spine, if you look down into the valley below you can see *Wheal Martin*, the *China Clay Museum*. If you want to visit for a greater exploration of the industry you will need to drive as there is no path down to it from here.

RIDGE RUNNING

5. Continue along the cycle path for about 400 yards at which point the path ends. Turn around and head back to the car by retracing your steps.

6. If you wish to extend this walk, then once back at your car, cross over the footbridge turn left towards a car park and then follow the instructions for the Eden Trail Walk 1.

LINKS:

A Brief History of China Clay
https://www.cornwalls.co.uk/history/industrial/china_clay.htm
The Clay Trails http://www.claytrails.co.uk/
Wheal Martin, China Clay Museum https://www.wheal-martyn.com/

PHOTO ALBUM:

https://flic.kr/s/aHskxe3CiH

7

PONTS MILL

BRIEF DESCRIPTION: A gorgeous woodland walk through a vanishing industrial landscape. Walk through the remnants of a tin and copper industry, that then moved into china clay back in the 1800s. To experience the modern china clay industry choose Walks 5 and 6. This walk offers great exercise for dogs as they rush up and down the hillsides.

LENGTH: 3 miles
EFFORT: Moderate
TERRAIN: Good footpaths, can be muddy
FOOTWEAR: Trainers or boots
LIVESTOCK: None
PARKING: Ponts Mill car park at the end of a no through road. PL24 2RR
WCs: None
CAFÉ / PUB: None
OS MAP: 107

NEARBY ATTRACTIONS: Fowey. Eden Project

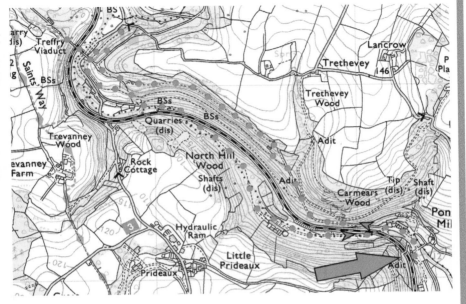

Elevation Profile

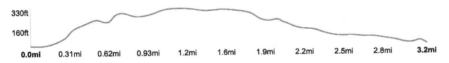

330ft										
160ft										
0.0mi	0.31mi	0.62mi	0.93mi	1.2mi	1.6mi	1.9mi	2.2mi	2.5mi	2.8mi	3.2mi

ABOVE THE TREETOPS ON THE VIADUCT

DIRECTIONS:

1. From the car park, with the river in front of you, turn left and walk upstream. Head towards the metal gates and walk through, passing the Luxulyan Valley notice board.

2. As the path veers left before the railway bridge, take the clear footpath on your right. Climb the few steps, go through a kissing gate and then start walking uphill. If you look down at the path you are walking on, you can see evidence of the *Carmears Inclined Plane* tramway. To the right of the path is a small stream and after heavy rain, you can spot lots of

Carmears Inclined Plane: This was a 1 in 9 horse-drawn tramway, driven by horsepower and the giant waterwheel at the top of the slope; it was used to bring the granite and china clay down off the hillside. Remains of the granite setts can still be seen at your feet.

Leats: A leat is a small canal; a man-made waterway created to deliver water to a particular

small waterfalls in the hillside to your right. After a climb, you will come to a stone bridge, just before it on the left is a small path, take this and then follow it onto and over the bridge. Now turn left and continue uphill.

3.   As you reach the small stream (*leat*), you will need to walk left, upstream. It doesn't matter which side of the bank you choose to walk. Your path now joins several others, there are two right-hand paths take the lower of the two. The leat should now be on your right and, shortly, the remains of the *Wheelpit Mill* although the wheel itself is no longer

location. The first leat you cross is the Fowey Console Leat and was built to supply water to the copper mines at Penpillick Hill. After you climb up the steps next to the waterwheel, and onto the top path, the leat that runs along this path is the Carmears Leat which was built to drive the waterwheel.

i **Wheelpit Mill:**
Originally built in 1841 the water from the Carmears Leat flowed over the top of the waterwheel and delivered

LOVED BY ALL DOGS

51

present. Walk along the path until you get to a massive *granite boulder* on top of the leat. Having examined it return to the waterwheel and take the steps to the right of the wheel. I would recommend putting dogs back on leads for this section, it is well fenced off but the drop is considerable.

4. At the top of the wheel take the footpath left. Dogs can come off the lead again now. This is the highest path in the Luxulyan Valley but can be prone to mud. Possibly because of the current closure of the top leat.

5. You will pass a stone with a K on one side and a T on the other. This is a boundary stone marking the boundary between land owned by Robert Treffry and Nicholas Kendall, although everything that you see on this walk is created by Treffry.

6. The path now comes out into a large open area and what appears to be a large stone wall. This is the top of the very impressive *Treffry Viaduct*, although at this angle you can't see it properly. Looking towards the viaduct, we will be turning right onto another path, however, it is well worth walking along the viaduct and back before doing so.

Crossing the viaduct is magnificent, with incredible views. Within the viaduct itself runs another leat, occasionally there are

the power to help the horses haul the wagons up the inclined plane. When the inclined plane was abandoned, two large grinding pans were employed to crush granite and extract the suspended china clay. This was transported, in a liquid form, down to the dries down by the valley floor.

i **Granite Boulders:** Along this walk, you will have to navigate huge granite boulders and you can see how earlier engineers dealt with some of them. If you examine the giant boulder by the waterwheel pit you can see a run of holes all lined up; these would have been made with tools called feathers & wedges, to calve off segments of rock. On this boulder, you can also see where it was successfully split for the leat. The boulders at Luxulyan are so exceptionally large that one was used to carve a sarcophagus for the Duke of Wellington's tomb in St Paul's Cathedral in the 1850s.

i **Treffry Viaduct:** Built by Richard Treffry in 1839, this viaduct is an engineering masterpiece. It has 10 arches, spanning 200 metres and stands 27 metres tall. The viaduct

HIDDEN BUILDINGS

gaps in the granite path where, if you peer through, you might be able to see water running. I would strongly recommend dogs on leads if you do walk along the viaduct, Harry once tried to jump up onto the wall. I nearly died. At the other side of the viaduct and to the left is another disused leat, this is the Charlestown Leat that was built by Charles Rashleigh in the 1790s, to provide water to his newly built harbour in Charlestown, almost four miles away. Once back onto this side of the viaduct turn left onto the path mentioned above.

7.   Follow this path, with the wall on your left and then go through the gap and down some steps. The path now runs down through a very picturesque beech wood towards the valley floor. It's easy to pretend you are in a fantasy film set, with giant granite boulders strewn across the floor. Cross a small footbridge over the leat and turn left on the footpath. The leat should now be on your left as you walk back toward the viaduct.

8.   Keep to this path until you reach a place where there is a field on either side of the path. Continue along the path until you get level with the end of the fields and then cross the stile on your right to enter that field. Head down to the bottom left corner, through a kissing gate and turn left onto the path.

9.   Follow this path down towards the

had a dual purpose, it was built to provide a tramway across the valley, but also to provide power to the waterwheel. Within the viaduct runs the Carmears Leat. You can sometimes see the water flowing beneath your feet. It is a stunning piece of architecture and is now a scheduled monument.

GREAT FOR EVERYONE

river. It will now take you all the way back to the car park, occasionally crossing over the river and under railway lines. Just over halfway, there is a well-preserved *china clay dry* complete with its chimney.

10. Continue along the path until you return to the start of the walk. There is a small stream just before the car park in which you can wash your dog.

China Clay Dry: It is cheaper and easier, due to the weight and fluidity of liquid, to dry the china clay as close to its extraction site as possible and so, in the past, dries were built alongside mining areas. China clay arrived in a suspended liquid form at the back of the dry; it was then spread over the coal-fired drying floor. The dry china clay was then shovelled forward to the linhay area and was taken away by cart, tram or lorry to the docks on St Austell Bay. This dry was called Trevanney Dry, it was built in 1920 and closed in 1965.

CLAY DRIES CHIMNEY

LINKS:

Luxulyan Valley http://www.luxulyanvalley.co.uk/

PHOTO ALBUM:

https://flic.kr/s/aHsmaY4bVU

8

IDLESS GUNPOWDER WALK

BRIEF DESCRIPTION: A short and enjoyable walk, there is the option to shorten it by a mile. You are bound to spot buzzards flying overhead as they look down on you exploring an ancient hillfort and gunpowder stores. There may be cyclists, but this is not a cycle network and there are no cliffs or livestock, making this a lovely walk for dogs to be off lead for the entire walk.

LENGTH: 3 miles. Option to shorten at two points
EFFORT: Easy to moderate
TERRAIN: Good footpaths
FOOTWEAR: Trainers or boots
LIVESTOCK: None
PARKING: Idless Forestry Commission car park. TR4 9QT
WCs: None
CAFÉ / PUB: Woodman's Cabin. They also have a little dog shower for muddy feet
OS MAP: 105

NEARBY ATTRACTIONS: Truro. Healey's Cornish Cider Farm

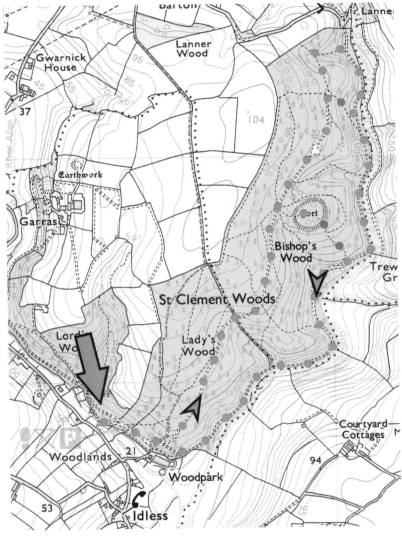

Elevation Profile

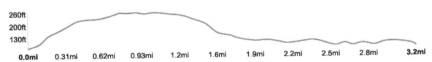

BUZZARD FLYING OVERHEAD

DIRECTIONS:

1. From the car park take the wide unmade road uphill.

2. Head uphill for just under a mile, carry on past a bench and some footpath signs and keep walking until the path starts to level out. Now start to look ahead and to your right and you will hopefully notice a large clump of trees that look different from all the other trees in the area. They are deciduous rather than coniferous and in a very obvious group. These trees mark the location of the *hillfort*. Keep walking until you are almost level with them and you will see three paths, all close to each other, to the right of the trail.

3. Take the middle path which will

Hillfort: This Iron Age hillfort sits in the middle of an ancient woodland once known as Bishop's Wood, created as a deer park by the Bishop of Exeter during the thirteenth century. When the wood was taken over by the Forestry Commission, it was replanted with a coniferous cash crop but thankfully the fort was protected. You can still see the two silver stars at both entrances, which were erected to remind the Commission where they couldn't cut and replant. The hillfort has never been investigated archaeologically but one day its

take you straight into the heart of the hillfort. If you find yourself bypassing the fort you have picked the wrong path. Stick to the path walking through the fort and you can clearly see the defensive ramparts and ditches.

If you wish to do the shorter walk, stay on this path as it heads downhill to the valley floor. You will rejoin the main walk at Step 6. Once on the valley floor turn left to explore the *Gunpowder Works*.

4.   Having explored the hillfort walk back up to the main trail and continue right. The views are lovely up here and the pine woods to the left of the path are lovely to wander in. The trail opens into a large clearing and then continues on.

secrets may be revealed.

i **Gunpowder Works:** Gunpowder was increasingly being used in the mining process but was a dangerous product to make. Gunpowder works were sited near rivers so that the powder could be kept damp and clothing washed down. Despite these precautions, explosions were a common occurrence. The Cornwall Blasting Powder Company began manufacturing gunpowder in Bishop's Wood in 1863. They moved into the buildings vacated by a former tin plant but sadly, it

RUINED GUNPOWDER STORES

REMAINS OF THE GUNPOWDER WORKS

After a short while, you reach a second clearing, not as obvious as the previous one.

5.   The large trail now peters out into a couple of smaller paths. If you want to cut down to the valley floor through the wood take the path to your right, if you want a slightly longer walk, take the path in front of you. This will head out of the woods and just as you reach a dip, turn right downhill, following the edge of the woods.

6.   You are now on the valley floor with the river running on your left. After half a mile, keep an eye out to your left, just after the river starts to split into several streams. Between the path and the river is a collection of abandoned buildings that were once part of a gunpowder works.

didn't get off to a good start following a "fearful explosion" in 1864 which killed and injured many factory girls. The works remained in operation but suffered from a shrinkage in business due to the contraction in the local mining industry, as well as a growing preference for dynamite. It was eventually broken up for scrap in 1887.

i **Eucalyptus Trees:** Planted in 1965 by the Forestry Commission, these are the remnants of a failed experiment, looking at eucalyptus as a cash crop.

A few yards on, the path coming down from the hillfort, rejoins the path you are now on. As you continue walking you might spot a grove of large *eucalyptus trees* to your right. A bit further on by the river bed is another collection of building foundations also belonging to the gunpowder works.

7.   Continue along the path until you return to your car park. As the path rises up, away from the river, this is your last chance to wash the dogs down before you get back to your car.

LINKS:

The Gunpowder Processs This link takes you to information about the larger Kennal Vale Gunpowder works, in Cornwall. https://www.cornish-mining.org.uk/

PHOTO ALBUM:

https://flic.kr/s/aHskAkevns

9

GRAMPOUND

BRIEF DESCRIPTION: A nice easy walk through country lanes, discovering little hamlets and fine country houses. This walk spans every historic age of Cornwall with evidence of Iron Age hillforts and Roman settlements as well as Domesday properties and medieval barns.

LENGTH: 5 miles
EFFORT: Easy
TERRAIN: Mostly country lanes. Some fields (avoidable) and tracks
FOOTWEAR: Any
LIVESTOCK: Cows but avoidable
PARKING: TR2 4RT
WCs: Grampound Community Centre
CAFÉ / PUB: Grampound Community Centre / The Dolphin Arms
OS MAP: 105

NEARBY ATTRACTIONS: Trewithen Gardens. Witch houses at Veryan. Lost Gardens of Heligan

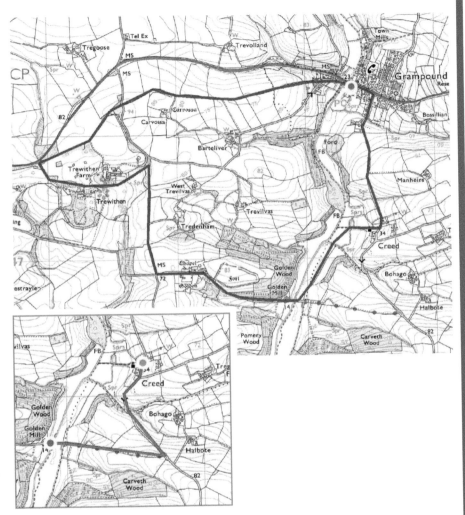

Elevation Profile

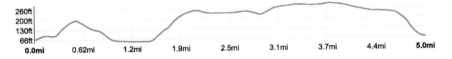

260ft								
200ft								
130ft								
66ft								
0.0mi	0.62mi	1.2mi	1.9mi	2.5mi	3.1mi	3.7mi	4.4mi	5.0mi

TREWITHEN ESTATE

DIRECTIONS:

1. From the *Grampound* car park, head towards the main road and turn right, walk along the road until you get to the turning on the right for Creed. Walk along this lane for just under a mile. After a quarter of a mile keep a look out for the remains of a mediaeval stone cross in the hedge-row on your left. All that is now left is the base and a hole where the upright would have stood, making it look like a well. This was one of a series of crosses linking Grampound and Creed. Continue along the road until you get to Creed. When you get to the main church gates on your right, you now have two options. The next section of the path is permissive

Creed Church: Some Norman construction can be seen but the majority of the church is from the fourteenth to sixteenth century, and it has good examples of mediaeval stained glass. In 1791 the Rector of Creed, William Gregor, discovered Titanium. Details of the discovery on the Lizard, are in the church.

Golden: A small but pretty hamlet, consisting of a farm, a well, a manor house and some very old buildings

and closed between Oct and Mar for the shooting season. There are also normally a lot of cows in the fields ahead. So take Option One to avoid cattle or if walking between Oct/Mar. See Grampound.

OPTION ONE

Avoiding fields. Continue walking along the road. Head uphill for about half a mile and then take an unmade road to your right. Ignore the track by the river and continue uphill. (If you get as far as the left-hand road junction you have just overshot the pathway.) There are lovely views from this high road, to your right you can just see *Creed Church* and ahead you can see a wood sheltering Golden Camp, an Iron Age hill fort. The Hill Fort must have had great views. It also sat above the River Fal, which was much wider and deeper than today. Now continue along the road, eventually, it will drop down and you will get to the River Fal. This is where Option Two joins the path. See Creed Church.

OPTION TWO

Closed October – March. Go through the church gates and take the path on the left of the church, follow it down to the fence on the left and then leave the churchyard. The path now goes through a spinney, for about 200 yards, it can be overgrown. The path now drops down to the left and over a small wooden bridge that spans a little stream. You are now in the first of two fields. The metal wires

incorporated into the farm. The building that looks like a chapel might be part of the old manor house and dates from around the sixteenth century.

Trewithen Estate: A large family home with Spring opening only. John Hawkins was the first member of the family to move to the county in 1554. Originally a courtier to Henry VIII, he settled at Trewinnard, near St Erth, married and established a maritime trading business through Mevagissey that thrived for many years. The current house was built in the seventeenth century.

Grampound: This has long been the site of an important settlement, from the Iron Age Hillfort, the Roman Settlement, the Domesday parish and the Mediaeval market to a Georgian and Victorian commercial centre. Sitting at the junction of one of Cornwall's principal routes with its great bridge providing the first crossing point over the River Fal, Grampound has a long and established history. Just in front

THE OLD MANOR AT GOLDEN

you need to duck under are electrified. It will give you a small tingle if you touch it. Head across the middle of the field to the gap in the hedge. You are now in a very long field, walk the length of it until you get to a five-bar gate at the other end. There are often cows in these fields. If cattle block your way you can take the footbridge over the River Fal into the next field and continue left towards the five-bar gate at the end of this field. (This is not the proper path, but if you suddenly need to avoid the cattle, it's an option.) Once you have left the field you are at the same point as the alternative option.

2.   Cross over the Fal via the road bridge and take the road uphill. There is a "pub" to your right but you won't get a drink here, it's a private building for the Estate Shoots. Walking on, you pass through the lovely hamlet of *Golden* and eventually reach a T-junction. From the River Fal to this T-Junction is about half a mile. Turn right and continue for another half a mile. This road can be busy so watch out for traffic as there are no pavements. After half a mile, take the left-hand turning into the grounds of *Trewithen Estate*. Stick to the main drive through the Estate passing the lake on your right and after a while Trewithen House itself on the left. If the gardens and cafe are open, this is a nice place to stop and explore. Trewithen is generally only opened in the Spring. See Golden and Trewithen Estate.

of St Nun's Church stands an impressive medieval cross. Hidden behind the main road and now redeveloped as homes, lies the site of Grampound Tannery, home to the highly sought after, Croggon leather.

3.   Continue along the main drive as it heads out to the main road. Pass through the Estate gate posts and cattle grid and then directly to your right you will see a white picket fence and a gate, go through the gate.

4.   You are now walking along what is considered to be a Roman road. This bridleway will take you back to the start of the walk. Like any good Roman road, this is a pretty straight path. Every time the path seems to turn to the right, ignore it and continue forward. Each of the right turns have Private signs, so you don't need to worry about getting lost. The path starts on grass, goes through a small copse, then crosses a minor road. There is no more traffic, after this point, and the path travels between fields. After you have crossed the road, the next turning on the right is towards a house called Carvossa. This is also the location of a Romano British site, Caerfos, archaeological studies show a settlement from 60 AD to the third century. although is visible today. When the path starts to head down the hill and under trees, you may want to get any dogs back on lead as you are about to head back into Grampound village. The path re-joins a village lane that heads down towards the main Truro road. Turn right and walk along the main road, over the river, and then back to where you began.

SUNSET OVER CARVOSSA

LINKS:

Golden https://bit.ly/2PIBl0O
Roman Settlement at Carvossa
https://historicengland.org.uk/listing/the-list/list-entry/1016890
Trewithen Gardens https://trewithengardens.co.uk/

PHOTO ALBUM:

https://flic.kr/s/aHsm4pNyxT

10

MEVAGISSEY & PENTEWAN

BRIEF DESCRIPTION: This is a great walk that follows the cycle path up towards Heligan. It then branches off across several fields with great views. The path then winds down into Pentewan, from there we follow the coast path home to Mevagissey taking in an abandoned set of pilchard stores. The last section is demanding.

LENGTH: 5 miles (alternate route adds 2 miles)
EFFORT: Strenuous in parts
TERRAIN: Hilly, fields, coast path, cycle path. Often muddy
FOOTWEAR: Walking boots. In dry weather trainers, etc. should be fine
LIVESTOCK: Cows likely - alternate route available
PARKING: Mevagissey Long Stay Car parks. Willow Carpark / Sunny Corner. PL26 6RZ
WCs: Mevagissey / Pentewan
CAFÉ / PUB: Mevagissey / Pentewan
OS MAP: 105

NEARBY ATTRACTIONS: Lost Gardens of Heligan. Charlestown Shipwreck Centre. Caerhays Castle

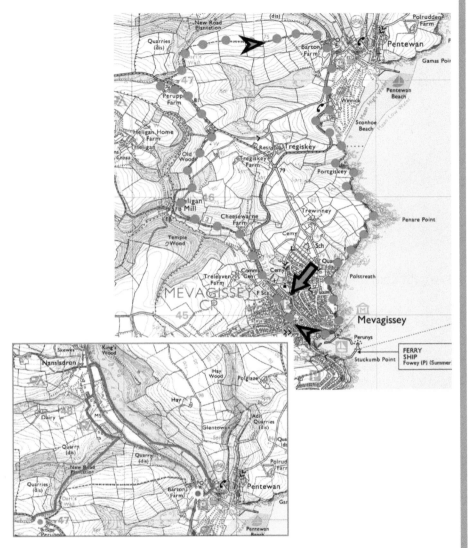

Elevation Profile

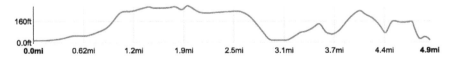

0.0mi	0.62mi	1.2mi	1.9mi	2.5mi	3.1mi	3.7mi	4.4mi	**4.9mi**

160ft

0.0ft

MEVAGISSEY HARBOUR

DIRECTIONS:

1. From your car park make your way onto the B3273, this is the main St Austell road leading out of the village. Head north in the St Austell direction. You will pass the bus stop and fire station, on your left, and as the road starts to head uphill, look to your left by the Mevagissey Community Centre. You will see signs to *Heligan* going via the National Cycle Path, route 3. Take this path.

2. Around your first mile, there is a footpath leading off towards Heligan; this is just as the cycle path turns right and starts to head uphill. Ignore this path and stay on the cycle trail for another mile. At first, there is a very steep section, and then the path levels out. After a while, the path will navigate an electricity sub-station,

Heligan: The Heligan Estate was first recorded in the 1200s, it was taken over by the Tremayne family, with the house that we see today, being built in the 1700s. The Estate grew and prospered until the start of the First World War. Then the Estate workers, along with many from the village, enlisted and went off to war. The villagers tended towards the Navy, but those from the Estate were land men and joined the army. The majority died, and the residing Tremayne owner moved to Italy, the Estate fell into neglect. The house was split into flats in the seventies, but the

and the path will then run alongside a road. See Heligan.

3. It will then start to pass along a collection of old farm buildings. As you pass the buildings, the path will begin to rise again turning left, at the point of the second left-hand bend you will leave cycle route 3. From the end of the farm buildings to this junction is approximately 30 yards. Your new path is off to the right and is often overgrown and poorly signed. You need to find the tall metal post on the left, pointing to Mevagissey and Pentewan. Directly to the right is your path. If you find yourself at a T-junction and to your right you are looking at a stone road bridge, you have overshot the path. Head back, although from this direction the new footpath is easier to see.

(If you wish to take the longer route or avoid the potential cows in the field ahead, this is the point when you need to follow the alternative route. Go to step 13.)

4. This is a short path that leads to the road so if you are walking with a dog, it's best to have them on a lead. At the road, cross directly over towards the unmade lane. There is a footpath sign to the right of this unmade lane. Follow this old road down to a five-bar gate. Regardless of whether the gate is open or not, climb over the granite stile to the left of the gate. Take this path, turning right through the woods, it will follow the edge of the

gardens continued to be neglected until Tim Smit and John Willis, one of the Tremayne family, started to explore the grounds following the 1990 hurricane. They discovered the bones of a wonderful Victorian Estate, with many of the features still standing, just. Over the next few decades, it has been restored and turned into the nation's favourite garden, regularly voted by the nation's favourite public garden.

Pentewan: As you walk across the fields, to the right, you are looking over St Austell Bay and Pentewan. Pentewan was first mentioned in 1086 in the Domesday Book and has continued as a small working village. It has benefited from having a local quarry extracting Pentewan Stone, tin extraction from the local river, being a major port for the china clay Industry with a railway line serving it from St Austell, and it has also been a home for fishing boats and the pilchard industry. Walking around the village, you will see many remnants of its long industrial heritage.

field and after 50 yards, climb over the granite stile to your right. You are now near the bottom of the field you just left. Continue along the edge of the field until you get to the bottom left corner of the next field.

5.   The walk now continues through five arable fields. The path cuts diagonally through the middle of the first three fields. It can seem a bit unnerving at first, especially in the winter months where the path isn't clear but head forward on a diagonal path and as you climb the field you will see the gap in the hedgerow ahead, walk towards that. It is easier to see the gap in the hedge in the next two fields.

During high summer the path is clear, but the views disappear as the crop, if corn, will be about 10 foot high. As you leave the third field, the path now follows along the right-hand edge of the field, with the hedge always on your right. Continue downhill into the fifth field, keeping the hedge on your right.

6.   Dogs on lead for the next few stages. At the bottom of the field, there is a five-bar gate with a kissing gate to the

Portgiskey: There is a small collection of pilchard cellars. Pilchard fishing was the main industry of St Austell Bay. For reasons that are unclear the pilchard began to turn up in our waters in vast numbers. The whole of the St Austell Bay benefited from this bounty, but it was Mevagissey that was pre-eminent in the fishing industry. Although not particularly popular in Britain, the pilchard was highly sought after on the continent. At one point in the early 1900s, the St Austell Bay area exported around 75 million pilchards. To process the fish, they were first salted in brine tanks and then packaged in wooden casks. The casks had holes in the bottom, and a lid was

PORTGISKEY COVE

left. There are usually cattle in the field. Check the tips in the front of this book for walking through cattle. The path is in the middle of the field and heads downhill and to the right. You are heading towards the large oak tree that you can see on your right as you pass through the gate. At the bottom of the field is another kissing gate that leads onto an old drive heading down towards the B3273. Cross over towards the Mill Garage and then follow the main road right, heading towards Mevagissey.

(This is where the alternate route rejoins the walk.)

7.   At this point, you can walk left into *Pentewan* for refreshments or a bit further on, turn left into Pentewan Sands, again for refreshments and a swim. Pentewan is the village. Pentewan Sands is a holiday park with a large sandy private beach. There is a dog ban for most of the year and no facilities in winter.

8.   Little Bay Café offer a free bottle of water on production of this walking guide. Cafe location at the end of the walk.

9.   The path now continues along the coast path. This is picked up just by the right-hand side of the white entrance gates to Pentewan Sands. It is signed for the Coast Path. The path heads inland for a while and then the path splits. Take the left-hand path over the stile and now

placed on top to which weights were added in order to squeeze the oil from the fish. To further leverage the squeeze, a long pole was slotted into the hole in the wall, and weights were tied to the end of it. The pole rested on top of the lid and pressed the pilchard. The lids were then fitted, and the barrels were shipped out.

COASTPATH FROM PENTEWAN

follow the path back to Mevagissey. Keep the sea on your left. If you find yourself on the footpath directly on the road, you have overshot the turning for the coast path.

10.   As the path heads back towards the sea, there is an option to head down to a small cove called *Portgiskey*. It is also possible to access Portgiskey from Pentewan Sands, avoiding the hill path, but this is only possible at an exceptionally low tide and may also involve some rock scrambling. See Portgiskey.

11.   The path then continues to Mevagissey and is quite arduous, with lots of ups and downs, although it is only about a mile. As the path heads into Mevagissey, you will begin to pass some gardens and a gate into Trevalsa Hotel on your right. Just after this, there is a path on your left down to Polstreath Beach. This is a lovely and often empty beach. Possibly because of the 100 steps.

12.   Continuing along the coast path you start to look down on the harbour of Mevagissey, carry on down through the tiny lanes and then rest.

BEAUTIFUL SCENERY

ALTERNATIVE ROUTE:

13. This adds an extra two miles but they are downhill and then flat. Do not leave the cycle path but continue on until you meet a T-junction, about 100 metres. Turn right and walk under the road bridge, follow this trail all the way down the hill. The cycle path follows the main road and then crosses over it. You will then follow the pavement for a few yards and then turn right over the river. Once you have crossed the bridge, turn right and walk downstream along the river. Take the large obvious left-hand path that leads into the woods. This will take you into Pentewan village. Pass the cycle hire shop and then you are back on a road. Turn right and walk along it until you get to the main road and the Mill Garage. At this point, you will re-join the original route at Step 7. See Pentewan.

WORKING BOATS

LINKS:

The Cornish Fishing Industry https://bit.ly/2Bnjbwr
A History of Pentewan http://www.pentewan.com/a-brief-history-1/
Little Bay Cafe https://bit.ly/2UVEyhs
The Lost Garden of Heligan http://heligan.com/the-story/introduction/

PHOTO ALBUM:

https://flic.kr/s/aHsm4pNyxc

11

TRELISSICK

BRIEF DESCRIPTION: A beautiful walk across parkland, fields and woodlands. The paths are well laid and, in many places, give excellent views across the large tidal rivers and estuaries. Along the way, the walk visits Roundwood Quays, an Iron Age hillfort hidden in the trees, and a beautiful river beach.

ADDITIONAL INFORMATION: Trelissick can also be approached by water via one of the many river taxis. The disembarkation is on part of the route. See Step 9.

LENGTH: 4.5 mile
EFFORT: Moderate
TERRAIN: River and woodland path
FOOTWEAR: Any
LIVESTOCK: Unlikely
PARKING: Trelissick National Trust car park. TR3 6QL
WCs: Trelissick
CAFÉ / PUB: Trelissick
OS MAP: 105

NEARBY ATTRACTIONS: Trelissick Gardens. Truro

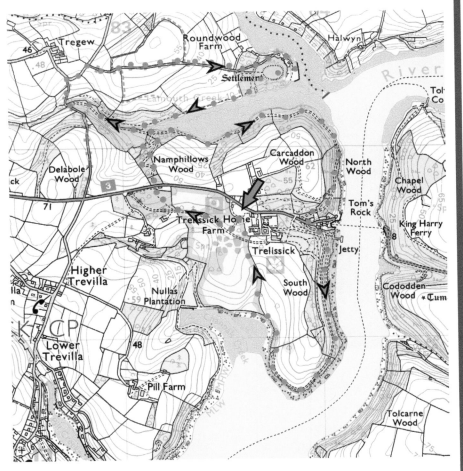

Elevation Profile

TRELISSICK HOUSE

DIRECTIONS:

1. From the car park head towards the information point and look for the fingerpost pointing to the Woodland Walks. Follow the sign to the black metal fence and go through the gate. Now turn immediately right and walk along the grass path through the parkland. You are heading towards the tree line at the top right-hand corner of the park. When you get to the trees, pass through the kissing gate and turn right in front of the ornamental gatehouse. The path now crosses a road, which can be busy, cross over and go through the next gate.

TRELISSICK TOWER

VIEWS TOWARDS CARRICK ROADS

2. Follow the path as it zigzags downhill with the occasional view over water. At the bottom, the path splits left and right. Turn left, almost immediately the path splits again. Ignore the right-hand path leading down to a bridge and continue left along this valley footpath.

3. When the footpath comes to a fence go through the gate and turn right, following the unmade road uphill. At the top, you will come out onto a quiet road. Turn right and walk along it until you reach an unmade road on your right, where you will see a fingerpost pointing towards the footpath. Head along this road for a short while, when it widens out, look to your left for a clear footpath leading into a

i **Trelissick House:** A stately home with a dramatic Palladian visage looking down over Carrick Roads. Built in 1755, the neo-classical pillars were added by Thomas Daniell in 1824.

i **Carrick Roads:** This enormous body of water is easily identified on any map of Cornwall. From its wide soft mud banks, it deepens to 46m and is heavily tidal, affecting all the many large rivers that flow into it. Because of this, the river banks are covered in mussels and

81

field. At this point there is an information board welcoming you to Roundwood and Tregew Meadows.

4.   This path passes down through two fields tracking the route of the unmade road. It is a good location for skylarks and you can often hear them singing overhead. The path rejoins the road and you should now continue along it down towards the Quay. Walk through the open gate and along the private driveway towards the front of the river and Quay.

5.   Having explored the Quay, locate the flight of granite steps by the large abandoned stone building and climb up into the hillfort.

6.   Although the hillfort is now completely overgrown with trees there are many paths through it that you can use to

seals and dolphins are regularly spotted. It is also a great location for migratory birds. The depth of the waters also makes it perfect for giant ocean tankers to dock for repairs, ocean liners to visit and the Royal Navy to undertake operations. Its military importance has always been apparent, and Henry VIII built two castles to protect the mouth of the waterway.

A roadstead (or roads - the earlier form) is a body of water sheltered from rip currents, spring tides or ocean swell where ships can lie reasonably safely at anchor without dragging or snatching. It is often used for ships waiting to enter ports and harbours.

explore. If your path cuts through a large mound you will be walking through one of the original walls. When you have finished exploring you need to make your way out of the fort, with the Quay behind you and the river on your left-hand side. To the far left by the river bank itself there are some uncomfortably high drops that are unfenced, so be aware. As you leave the fort you need to be at the bottom left-hand corner by a large sloping field and an Information Board. By the path is a small granite marker with two pink arrows. You now need to take the footpath that leads away from the fort, alongside the river.

7.   Follow this path until it heads down towards a decorative footbridge and follow the path left. Shortly you will arrive at the junction you were at, at Step 2. Ignore your two previous paths and now take the main path left, walking back along the river's edge. As you walk along, if you look over to your left you will soon see the hillfort and Quay across the water.

8. This section of path is well made and takes you to the King Harry Ferry. At one point the footpath splits, take the left-hand fork and continue until you get to the road. The path continues directly across the road but, if you wish, you can go down to the river for a bit and watch the ferry. There is a nice viewing platform down to the left of the road through a small lawned area.

9. Continuing along the path you cross the footpath leading from the passenger ferry to the gardens. Keep to the path labelled Woodland Walk. This path now loops around the bottom of Trelissick gardens and estate.

10. When you get to a black metal fence, go through the gate and savour the views. Above you, to the right sits *Trelissick House* enjoying incredible views. To your left you are looking down towards *Carrick Roads*, in the distance on the horizon you can spot the round shape of Pendennis Castle sitting above Falmouth Harbour. If the tide is low there is a nice beach to play on.

11. Now walk up the park, towards the house. The path will take you right to the top of the hill and back to where you first started by the car park.

SUB-TROPICAL PLANTS

LINKS:

Trelissick
https://www.nationaltrust.org.uk/trelissick

PHOTO ALBUM:

https://flic.kr/s/aHsmxsCf3C

<u>12</u>

ST ANTHONY'S HEAD

BRIEF DESCRIPTION: A lovely walk around one of the
Roseland's headlands taking in St Anthony's Lighthouse,
Place House and St Anthony's Church, exploring the
beautiful Cornish creeks and coast. Dogs are on leads for
sections of this walk, and although there are often cattle,
it is a really lovely walk and gives everyone a really good
stretch.

LENGTH: 7 miles
EFFORT: Moderate
TERRAIN: Coast path
FOOTWEAR: Walking boots
LIVESTOCK: Cattle possible
PARKING: Porth National Trust car park. TR2 5EX
WCs: Towan Beach / St Anthony's Head
CAFÉ / PUB: Towan Beach – seasonal
OS MAP: 105

NEARBY ATTRACTIONS: Falmouth (via boat). Veryan witch
houses. St Mawes Castle

Elevation Profile

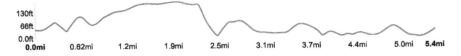

130ft									
66ft									
0.0ft									
0.0mi	0.62mi	1.2mi	1.9mi	2.5mi	3.1mi	3.7mi	4.4mi	5.0mi	5.4mi

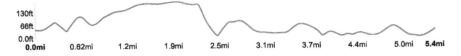

NORMAN CHURCH DOOR

DIRECTIONS:

1. From the car park head down to the beach going through the cluster of National Trust buildings. When you get to the coast path turn right and walk to St Anthony's Head. This is a two-mile section with two stiles, a potential for cattle and some high cliffs. The advice is to keep dogs on a lead. This section of coastline is very scenic

St Anthony's Lighthouse: Fans of Fraggle Rock will recognise St Anthony's Lighthouse from the opening sequences. Whilst the lighthouse is now a holiday let, the light and foghorn are still operational but automated. This is an incredibly

ST ANTHONY'S LIGHTHOUSE

and if you are lucky, you should spot seals surfing in the waves.

2.   After a mile and a half, the land to your right drops away and you can see over to Falmouth. Soon after that, you will get to St Anthony's Head. Here the path appears to fork, take the left-hand path and looking down to your left you should see a bird hide in the cliffs below. The path now heads through a defensive wall and you will find yourself in *St Anthony Head Battery*. Have an explore and then make your way to the front of the residential single-story buildings.

3.   The coast path continues to the left of the road in front of the residential properties. Follow the path with the metal handrail down the hillside. There is an option, halfway down, to turn left and visit the Battery Observation Post and the Bird Hide, the views from both these spots are excellent. Return to this point and continue down the steps. At the end of the handrail, you can turn left to view *St Anthony's Lighthouse*, although it is private and can only be viewed from a distance. Otherwise turn right.

4.   Dogs are fine off the lead for the next section. Keep on the footpath until you see a collection of large pine trees ahead. This section is very scenic but the path gets close to the edge again, so best to have dogs back on leads. After you have

PLACE HOUSE

cleared all the pines, the path now heads into fields and so long as these are clear of cattle, dogs will be fine off the lead. The views to your left overlook a large section of water called Carrick Roads, the large town opposite is Falmouth with *Pendennis Castle* to the left edge. As you walk along you will spot a twin castle on the edge of another land mass, this is *St Mawes Castle*.

5. As you walk past a beach there is a wood ahead of you, the path heads uphill to a signed gate in the top corner of the field. You are now entering a conservation area so dogs will need to go back on the lead.

6. Follow the path as it joins a private lane. The coast path now skirts behind *Place House* but the signage is clear as the path leaves the lane. It now goes past *St Anthony-in-Roseland Church* which is a lovely place to visit and then continues out onto a small road where you turn left and head down to the water.

7. When you get to the water's edge follow the signpost to Place Ferry. The coast path now continues across the water via the Ferry but we continue along the footpath into the woods.

8. The next mile and half is mostly in woodland so is safe to have your dogs off their leads. Keep the water on your left at all times and ignore any right-hand footpath signs to Borhotha. At the end

busy stretch of water as you can probably see for yourself, from traditional red-sailed Falmouth oyster boats to Ocean going liners and supertankers. In the middle of the bay sits Black Rock and further down the coast lurk the Manacles, a low-lying collection of rocks responsible for hundreds of shipwrecks over the centuries. The lighthouse was built by the Admiralty in 1835, replacing previous beacon fires.

 St Anthony-in-Roseland Church: Nicolas Pevsner, in his catalogue of the finest buildings in the English counties, considered St Anthony to be the best example of a twelfth century parish church, in Cornwall. Originally it was part of a larger Priory but that's long gone. There is a beautiful Norman door at the entrance and although it was modernised and restored in the nineteenth century much of the original building remains. One of the side doors leads directly into Place House a private residence that overlooks Cellars Beach.

 Place House: Place was built in 1861 by Sir

TOWAN BEACH

Thomas Spry in the style of a French chateau. He was also responsible for restoring St Anthony's Church and this was no doubt when the door to the church from the house was added. The church originally belonged to a Priory which has long gone. Place Ferry connected this remote section of the Roseland to the rest of the peninsula, estate workers from Falmouth and St Mawes would come across to work. As the estate wound down the ferry was abandoned until the establishment of the South West coast path when it was resurrected.

of this section, you will come to a long wooden bridge over a stream and boggy area. There is a road on the other side of this bridge, so dogs back on leads. Once across the bridge turn right and head back to your car. There are two car parks near each other, if you didn't park in this one just walk up the road and the second car park is on your right.

(i) **Pendennis Castle / St Mawes Castle:** Henry VIII built these twin castles to defend Carrick Roads from invasion. Whilst the cannon fire from one side wouldn't protect the whole entrance, twin fire covered the whole waterways. This was an important stretch of water both from the Channel and the Atlantic and was vulnerable to attack due to its size.

LINKS:

The National Trust at Porth
https://www.nationaltrust.org.uk/porth
St Anthony Head Battery
https://bit.ly/2EqzlZd

PHOTO ALBUM:

https://flic.kr/s/aHsm5enf9Q

EXTRA HELPINGS

I SPY

CELTIC CROSS

In some spots of Cornwall, you could trip over these, there are so many. They come in all shapes and guises but very few are a straight cross shape. In the past, they were moved around a lot and were also re-used as footbridges, foundation stones or gate posts, as well as cattle rubs.

GRANITE TOR

Weather erosion has created these incredible structures on the top of some hills. These are strangely shaped boulders, perching on top of each other. Bonus points if you find one with a Logan Stone. This is a rock that rocks and pivots when you stand on it.

WIND TURBINE

Over the past few years, these giant white turbines have popped up all over the landscape.

DRIES

An industrial building used in the processing of china clay, this will be an exceptionally large, long, low structure with a massive chimney at either one, or both, ends. Usually it will be hidden under years of trees and ivy, or alternatively converted into flats.

ENGINE HOUSE

A tall upright building with a massive chimney on one side. Easily spotted due to their isolation and height. Engine houses are most commonly associated with tin mines, they were used to pump water out of the shafts below ground. Some of the mines even run below the seabed.

CASTLE

We have several castles in Cornwall and most of them seem to be round. As well as Norman and Tudor castles we also have ancient hillforts including the legendary birthplace of King Arthur.

LIGHTHOUSE

Some of our lighthouses were built simply as automated lights, some, however, were once occupied. The Lizard Lighthouse was the last one to remain manned and was only switched to an automated system in 1998. Many have now been turned into holiday homes.

CHOUGH

Easily distinguished by their bright red beaks and feet, and their aerobatics Cornwall's national bird can be found mainly on the cliffs to the west of the county. At one point they disappeared from our shores altogether and only recently has a group started to re-colonise the county to the extent that they are now starting to spread slowly but surely east.

BUZZARD

A large brown, bird of prey, often mistaken for an eagle but we don't have any of them. If you see crows or gulls mobbing a larger bird it will probably be a buzzard. Keep an eye out for telegraph poles as they like to perch there.

MUSSELS

One of nature's natural bounties and the easiest shellfish to identify with their long blue-black oval cases. Archaeological records show that we have been eating mussels for the past 20,000 years.

CRAB

Fresh or on the fish stand, either will do. A popular summer activity is crabbing from a harbour wall, although you will never catch a crab large enough to eat. Get a line with a hook on the end and pierce on a bit of bacon, drop it in the water. Lo and behold, a few minutes later you'll have hooked a crab. Have a look, then throw it back in the sea.

SEAWEED

Well, what's the fun in not having an easy one to spot? Most seaweed is actually edible, in fact, several places in Cornwall now have it on the menu. Order some, it's really tasty.

SEAL

Like cows and dogs, seals are friendly and curious. They often come into harbours for easy food and to have a nose about. Out on coastal walks, they will often pop up if they hear new sounds. They seem to like listening to singing.

FOXGLOVE

These lovely tall pink spires herald early summer and grow wild across Cornwall. The Cornish hedgerows are a sight to behold in spring, although you wouldn't want to bump into one as they are actually granite walls wrapped in earth and plants.

SURFBOARD

We've been surfing in Cornwall ever since St Piran arrived in Cornwall, surfing in on a millstone, from Ireland. Surfing gained mass appeal at the beginning of the twentieth century using boogie boards or belly boards. It didn't take long before people switched over to standing up on much larger boards. Bonus points if you spot an old-style wooden boogie board.

FISHING BOAT

Another easy spot but see if you can identify some of the registrations. FY means the vessel was registered in Fowey. PW is Padstow, PZ is Penzance, SC is the Scilly Isles, SS is St Ives and FH is Falmouth. Bonus points for TO, which is Truro.

CORNISH LANGUAGE

The best place to spot this is on road signs but have a look around, you'll find it in all sorts of places. The language died out in 1770 but following a concerted effort, there are now several hundred Cornish speakers, although as yet, there are no native speakers. Give it time.

PASTY

A shy beast and often misrepresented. In the past, a pasty was a worker's lunch and was filled with whatever was to hand, including fish or fruit. Today, a traditional pasty is filled with steak, taken from the skirt cut of beef, swede, potatoes, onion, salt, butter and pepper. Nothing else. It must also be crimped on the side, not over the top. The pasty has even got a protected specialist status, detailing these features.

THE HISTORY OF CHINA CLAY IN CORNWALL

In the late sixteenth century, traders from the far east began to bring home beautiful cups and plates made from exquisite porcelain. To a continent that was used to pottery and stoneware, these pieces were treasures to be desired. The items were as thin and light as bones, they rang when you struck them, and the light shone through them. And yet they were strong enough to eat and drink from.

The British couldn't get enough of these expensive imports and acquiring them was the ultimate display of wealth and privilege. William Cookworthy was aware that if he could only find kaolin, the main component of porcelain, in the UK he would be sitting on a goldmine. He searched the country and in 1746 finally found a clay deposit of a similar standard to the Chinese kaolin, here in Cornwall. Earning it the nickname of china clay.

If the Chinese product was finer, this was disregarded, and the Cornish market exploded. A deposit north of St Austell was revealed to be one of the largest in the world, and a global industry began to rapidly develop.

The material didn't require deep mining, like tin or copper, and was retrieved using opencast mining. It was then blasted with water cannons, to separate the soft clay from the decomposing granite. The water turned white and ran off into the rivers, and as it ran down into St Austell Bay, the whole sea would turn white. Even in the 1970s, locals remember swimming in milky white water. For each tonne of clay extracted, there were five tonnes of mica waste. When the two materials were separated, the slag was taken and dumped back on the land, in long hills or in large conical structures. These large white hills were soon referred to as the Cornish Alps or Pyramids and rapidly changed the local skyline. Finally, the good wet clay was recovered and laid out in massive long low buildings, known as dries. With a chimney at each end, heat was run along the base and the clay above would slowly be dried out. Women, known as bal maidens, would shape and turn the mixture until it resembled dry blocks, that could be cut and easily transported up country and overseas to the waiting mills. This industry far outperformed fishing or farming and there wasn't a single family that wasn't in some way impacted by the new industry.

Leats (small canals) were laid out across the land to provide water directly to the source, and water wheels were built to power the engineering processes. The entire land in this area was covered in dries, villages grew up, simply to extract the clay. Initially, these dries were built right near the extraction points, but gradually as the railways were built, the wet sludge was transported to the docks at Charlestown, Pentewan and eventually the processing industry was consolidated at the large docks at Par. The expansion of the industrial developments in mid-Cornwall was all to further the china clay business. Over the centuries, vast fortunes were made. Over 250 years, 170 million tonnes of china clay was produced. 70% of this production was exported overseas, making Cornwall the pre-eminent global source of china clay.

China clay was in great demand and not just because of its use in the porcelain industry but because of its other properties. Not only is china clay able to deliver the finest finish to a product, it can also be eaten without any side effects. Thus, it is an integral part in the manufacture of consumable medicines. Any pill you have ever swallowed is coated in china clay to help it go down better. The chances are, that every single day, you come into contact with china clay in one shape or another.

Looking about you today every strange hill you see, will be a slag heap. The large pyramid towering over St Austell is now only vaguely white, but it must have been an incredible sight before nature began to reclaim it. Some of the heaps have been flattened and terraformed providing excellent walks and bike rides, and if you look at the ground you will see that, rather than soil, it is made up of a gritty mica residue. Strange buildings are hidden under trees and ivy, others, that have been restored, can be explored in safety. Some areas of the terraformed land still seem reminiscent of an alien planet. Others are more established, with the flora and fauna smoothing over the harsh scars on the landscape. Across the countryside large lakes are now present where the miners dug down to extract the raw material. In other areas there are large shallow pans of water, full of strange glowing green water, each pan a slightly different shade, covering many acres. The world-famous Eden Project is built in a clay pit, showing the ingenuity of mankind to reuse the land.

Nowhere in mid-Cornwall is untouched. Although the industry is still active here, it has declined with the discovery of a massive deposit in Brazil. The industry has moved to a fresher source, that is easier to extract with cheaper labour costs. It is hard to look around at some of the towns and villages today and appreciate that these were once the white-hot hubs of industry at the top of a global market. A time when Cornwall led the world.

THE TALE OF BOLSTER THE GIANT

or

What happens when you annoy a Saint

The Giant Bolster, striding from the Beacon to Carn Brea —
— a distance of six miles —

There is something about the landscape of St Agnes that invites larger than life tales. Here, a most unpleasant giant mistreats his wife and moons after a local saint. Boy did he pick the wrong woman to mess with...

Once upon a time, many years ago in the lands to the far west, where the sun sets on sea monsters and fairies, there lived a vicious giant. The name of this foul-tempered giant was Bolster and he lived by a village near the sea. The local people were so fed up with his behaviour that they built an enormous wall to try and keep him out. However, Bolster was so huge that he just laughed at their efforts and stepped over it. In fact, Bolster was so tall that in one stride he could step from the beacon above the village to the hill at Carn Brae some six miles away.

As Bolster roamed the land, he would go out of his way to stamp on the crops in the fields. He would kick over hedges so that the cows and sheep would wander out and the poor herders would have to spend days trying to gather them all back in. He would stride into the sea, grab the tails of grampus and throw them far out to sea, which is why you don't see them around the coast of Cornwall any more. They were so fed up of his ways that they all swam off and vowed not to return until the sun set in the east.

When Bolster wasn't terrorising the local population and wildlife he was making life miserable for his wife. If he was bored, he would tell her to carry rocks all the way up from the beach and surrounding fields, to the top of the nearby hill. This poor woman not only suffered from Bolster's constant harrying, but also from the fact that she was often unnamed, only being referred to as Bolster's wife, twice unlucky, therefore. As it happened, her name was Gonetta and whilst she was also a giant she wasn't anywhere near as tall or as strong as Bolster, and she would struggle to drag these stones to the top of the hill.

One day, bored with setting fire to the local heather, Bolster came to see how his wife was doing. As he arrived, he was furious to see she was sat down, laughing and chatting with another woman. As he strode over, ready to drag her by her hair back to the beach, he looked at the other woman and was struck dumb. He had never seen such beauty and was entranced. However, this is not a tale where love conquers all. Bolster's heart was not softened, he did not mend his ways. Instead, he began to pester Agnes, for that was this beauty's name. He continued to beat his wife, torment the villagers and terrorise the livestock but now he also mooned after Agnes, following her everywhere, and giving her no peace. She told him to leave her alone nicely, she told him at the top of her voice, she pleaded with him. She told him she might like him more if he changed his behaviour. Nothing worked. He would bang on the windows in the night so that he could see her face. He would drag her out of church so that he could talk to her, and when she sat down to eat, he would take her food for himself so that she didn't get fat. In every way that he could be annoying, he was. Agnes was beside herself and also pretty hungry. Not only was she fed up with how he treated her, but she could also see that his attentions to her were as nothing to his behaviour of others. Poor Gonetta and the long-suffering villagers, not to mention the creatures of the fields and seas.

Finally, Bolster removed Agnes's shoes. He declared that if she didn't have shoes, she wouldn't be able to walk. She would always be in her house, whenever he wanted to visit. Agnes, however, was not going to be stopped by such a mean move and spent the next day walking around the area, as usual, helping those that needed it. The villagers she met pitied her and bravely offered her their footwear, but she knew if she said yes, he would simply come and stamp on their homes with them inside. That night, as Agnes went to sleep with bruised and bloodied feet, she decided to put an end to Bolster and his horrible ways.

Agnes had long lived in the area and knew it very well, she realised that she knew something that Bolster didn't. The following morning, she told everyone to meet her on the cliffs above the beach, and when Bolster came hunting her out, she called up to him.

"Bolster. I have decided to set you a challenge. If you complete this challenge, as these villagers are my witnesses, I shall be your wife." It mattered not to Bolster that he already had one wife. "However, if you accept this challenge and fail, then you must leave this land and walk to the west, into the sea and never return. Again, the villagers will witness your promise." Now a promise in front of witnesses was a solemn thing so Bolster thought about it. One thing that Bolster wasn't, was particularly clever, and this made him cross when he thought people were trying to trick him.

"Do you think I'm stupid, woman? I won't make a promise if I don't know the terms of the deal!"

Agnes looked deflated. "Very well, you are too clever for me. This is the wager. Do you see this hole here?" and she pointed to a small hole in the ground by her feet. "My challenge is that you fill this hole with your blood."

Now Bolster laughed really loudly and to celebrate he caught two passing choughs that were flying past and tore their wings off.

"This is an easy challenge. I accept."

Agnes quickly recovered from her own deflated demeanour. "In front of witnesses?" She had been having second thoughts about her plan but as she looked on the corpses of the two birds, her kind heart stiffened.

"In front of witnesses, I solemnly pledge." In his mind, he knew he would win this bet, but he also knew that if he didn't, that he had no intention of leaving the village. What he didn't know was that Agnes also knew this.

Kneeling in front of the hole, Bolster took out his knife and cut his forearm and as the blood poured out, he held it over the hole and watched, with everyone else, as it poured into the small hole. After a few seconds Bolster was surprised and a bit perturbed to see that the little hole was not yet full, the plants around it remained green. However, he couldn't let the villagers see he was concerned, so he continued to brag about how easy this was and how he would make them all pay for doubting his ability. Minutes passed and still the hole hadn't filled and now Bolster was finding himself a little light-headed, so he lay down alongside the hole, with his arm over it. He was certain that any second now the little hole would be full and then he would make Agnes his wife.

Now, what Bolster didn't know but Agnes did, was that this hole went all the way down to the cliffs on the beach below. Bolster's blood was pouring down the hole, over the rocks and flowing out into the great sea beyond.

After a few more minutes Bolster stopped bragging, and after another few minutes, he stopped breathing as well, as the last drop of his blood flowed out and into the sea below.

When the villagers realised that their torment had finally come to an end they threw a great party. Gonetta skipped across the hills and carried nearby villagers over the fields to also join in the celebrations and Agnes danced until dawn, in her lovely soft shoes.

An enjoyable and gory tale, and a stark reminder to tread lightly and leave people's shoes alone.

SEASONAL RECIPES

There's nothing nicer than foraging for your own supper. Here are some of my favourite, and easiest recipes, from the most obvious and abundant foods you can find whilst out walking. These recipes are all rough and ready, food should be more freestyle.

SPRING – *Nettles*

Nettles are the bane of a walker's life but in early spring they are a tasty treat packed full of iron. Generally, people make a wonderfully vivid soup out of them, but I was passed this recipe from an old lady who I used to meet whilst walking our dogs. She swore that the new nettle shoots gave her strength for the year ahead.

RECIPE: *Stuffed Chicken Thighs*

Chop up an onion and bits of bacon and fry them in butter. Now, open up a boneless chicken thigh. Pack it with the mixture and a small handful of very young nettle shoots, removing any tough stalks. Don't worry about being stung, that goes when the nettles are cooked. Sprinkle over some oats, dried marjoram, salt and pepper, and a small knob of butter. Roll the thigh back up and tie up with string, to stop the contents falling out. Sprinkle some salt on the skin and then roast for around 40 minutes. Delicious.

SUMMER – *Elderflower*

Once you find a good elderflower patch, mark it well and come back to it again in autumn for the berries. In the spring the large white flouncy flower caps can be picked and turned into a delicious drink, either as a cordial or as champagne. Make sure you don't remove all the flower heads. Not everyone recognises elderflower. Just remember it's a bush or a tree. Large white flower heads growing up from the floor on a single stem are usually cow parsley.

RECIPE: *Elderflower champagne*

This is great fun and incredibly simple to make. There is a chance that the bottles may explode so use plastic bottles and store them somewhere, where they won't cause a problem. I follow the BBC recipe. Take a nice clean bucket, fill it with 4 litres of hot water and stir in 700g of sugar. When the sugar has dissolved, add the juice and zest of four lemons and two tablespoons of white wine vinegar. Then add 15 elderflower heads in full bloom, stir, cover with a towel and put aside for a day or two. Check if the mixture is becoming frothy, if it's not, add a pinch of dried yeast. Set aside for a few more days then strain and bottle in sterilised bottles. The Groslch ones are good or the 2lt fizzy drink bottles. Fill the bottles up leaving a good inch at the top and seal and store in a cool dry place. Drinkable after a week. If using plastic bottles keep an eye on how "tight" the bottle is becoming and release the cap a millimetre to reduce the pressure.

Even if you don't get the elderflower to ferment you will still have a lovely elder-flower drink.

AUTUMN – *Mushrooms*

First rule, if you aren't 100% certain of the identity, don't eat it. Wild mushrooms are an incredible treat and worth getting into. The easiest of all mushrooms to identify are Giant Puffballs. Quite simply they are large, white solid balls, about the size of a football, sometimes much larger. Usually growing in grass in early autumn. Nothing else looks remotely similar. Another very tasty mushroom that has no nasty lookalikes is the Cauliflower Fungus, found in conifer forests at the base of trees. Tricky to clean and best eaten young, not yellow and decaying.

RECIPE: *Simple mushrooms*

Slice, then fry in salt, butter and maybe a bit of garlic. Nothing more complicated than that. I love going on a morning walk and coming home with breakfast.

WINTER – *Mussels*

Mussels can be eaten at most times of the year but it's lovely to have such a tasty harvest in the bleakest months. Mussels should be avoided if there isn't an R in the month which is just another way to say avoid picking in the hotter months when the shells could form bacteria in the sun. Pick at low tide, go right down to the water's edge, this is where the largest mussels are, and don't pick anything shorter than an inch. If you pick at low tide at the furthest edge, then your harvest will have spent most of its time under water, rather than exposed to the sun. Pick and choose, do not clear out a patch. When you get home, empty them into a large container of water, discard any that open. Clean your mussels by yanking out the beard. This is the piece of seaweed that the mussel anchored itself to the rocks with. You may have removed these when you picked them, either way, you don't want to cook or eat them.

RECIPE: *Mussels PDQ*

Clean the mussels, removing the beard and put them in water. Put to one side until ready to cook. Now finely chop a bunch of shallots (or onions or leeks) and fry them gently in butter. Add the mussels and pour over wine or cider, and cover with a tight lid. You need enough liquid to give a depth of around one centimetre. You are not trying to boil them, you are steaming them. After five to ten minutes, serve! Bin any mussels that didn't open. Pour the cooking liquid over the mussels and maybe serve with chopped parsley and crusty bread. Proper fast food.

RECOMMENDED READING

Reading a story set in the place where you are staying / living, always adds an extra something. When the author describes a scene, you are instantly drawn into the book, especially when you can actually see it, not just imagine it! The following great stories are all set in this area and make for a great read.

Fault Line - Robert Goddard

Up with the Larks - Tessa Hainsworth

The Camomile Lawn - Mary Wesley

Over Sea, Under Stone – Susan Cooper

The Lost Years – EV Thompson

Rebecca – Daphne du Maurier

One Cornish Summer - Liz Fenwick

The House on the Strand – Daphne du Maurier

Castle Dor – Arthur Quiller-Couch & Daphne du Maurier

OS Map 104

OS Map 105

OS Map 106

OS Map 107

MORE BY LIZ HURLEY
Cornish Walks Series

WALKING IN THE MEVAGISSEY AREA
9780993218033 https://amzn.to/2FsEVXN
WALKING IN THE FOWEY AREA
9780993218040 https://amzn.to/2r6bDtL
DOG WALKS BETWEEN TRURO AND FOWEY
9780993218057 https://amzn.to/2jd83tm
TOP WALKS IN MID CORNWALL
9780993218064
TOP WALKS IN EAST CORNWALL
TOP WALKS IN WEST CORNWALL

A HISTORY OF MEVAGISSEY

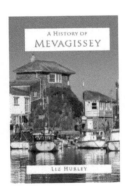

An engaging and informative history of Mevagissey.

For over eight hundred years, Mevagissey has flourished beside the south Cornish coastline. It was, in its heyday, a globally significant port, lighting the streets of London in the eighteenth century and feeding the homes of Europe. It has been battered by freak storms and a cholera out-break but has continued, unbroken, contributing in no small part to the colonisation of the world by Cornish men and women.

This potted history gives an insight into the history of the village and takes a humorous look behind the scenes, revealing what it is like to actually live and work in Cornwall's second largest fishing port. It debunks a few myths and introduces some lively, tall tales, as told through local voices.

Available in bookshops.
Paperback: 978-0993218026
Digital: https://amzn.to/2r5VlkA

SCRIBBLES FROM THE EDGE

When everyday life is anything but every day.

Liz Hurley gathers together her newspaper columns to deliver a collection of fast, funny reads. Join in as you share the highs and lows of a bookseller, dog lover and mother in Britain's finest county. This treasure trove of little gems moves from lifestyle pieces on living day-to-day behind the scenes in the UK's number one tourist destination, to opinion pieces on education, current affairs, science, politics and even religion. Watching the sun set over a glowing beach isn't quite so much fun when you are trying to find the keys your child hid in the sand, and the tide is coming in! Join in and discover just how hard it is to surf and look glamorous at the same time. Batten down the hatches as she lets off steam about exploding cars and rude visitors. Laugh along and agree or disagree with Liz's opinion pieces, as you discover that although life might not be greener on the other side, it's a lot of fun finding out.

Available in bookshops.
Paperback: 978-0993218002
Digital: https://amzn.to/2ji2UQZ

LOSING IT IN CORNWALL

The second collection of columns from Liz Hurley, still scribbling away on the edge. Still trying to hold it together. From serious to silly her columns cover all that life throws at us. A perfect selection of little titbits, to pick up and put down or read straight through.

Available in bookshops.
Paperback: 978-0993218019
Digital: https://amzn.to/2r4eHGG

HELLO AND THANK YOU

Getting to know my readers is really rewarding, I get to know more about you and enjoy your feedback; it only seems fair that you get something in return so if you sign up for my newsletter you will get various free downloads, depending on what I am currently working on, plus advance notice of new releases. I don't send out many newsletters, and I will never share your details. If this sounds good, click on the following: www.lizhurleywrites.com

I'm also on all the regular social media platforms so look me up.
#lizhurleywrites
#dreamingofcornwall

GET INVOLVED!

Join Walkers Talk Back on Facebook, to read about the next book in the walking series. Suggest routes, give feedback, receive advance copies. Better yet, share photos and feedback of the walks you enjoyed.
https://www.facebook.com/groups/841952742623247/

Did you enjoy this book? You can make a big difference.

Reviews are very powerful and can help me build my audience. Independent authors have a much closer relationship with their readers, and we survive and thrive with your help.

If you've enjoyed this book, then please let others know.

If you read it online leave a review on the site where you purchased it

Thanks for helping,
Liz